Making Meaning of Loss

Making Meaning of Loss

Change and Challenge Across the Lifespan

Richard L. Hayes

LEXINGTON BOOKS
Lanham • Boulder • New York • London

Published by Lexington Books
An imprint of The Rowman & Littlefield Publishing Group, Inc.
4501 Forbes Boulevard, Suite 200, Lanham, Maryland 20706
www.rowman.com

86-90 Paul Street, London EC2A 4NE

British Library Cataloguing in Publication Information Available

Library of Congress Cataloging-in-Publication Data

Names: Hayes, Richard L. (Richard Lee), 1946- author.
Title: Making meaning of loss : change and challenge across the lifespan
  / Richard L. Hayes.
Description: Lanham : Lexington Books, [2023] | Includes bibliographical references
  and index.
Identifiers: LCCN 2022042778 (print) | LCCN 2022042779 (ebook) |
  ISBN 9781666924503 (cloth) | ISBN 9781666924510 (ebook)
Subjects: LCSH: Loss (Psychology) | Bereavement--Psychological aspects. | Life
  cycle, Human.
Classification: LCC BF575.D35 H49 2023 (print) | LCC BF575.D35 (ebook) | DDC
  155.9/37–dc23/eng/20220921
LC record available at https://lccn.loc.gov/2022042778
LC ebook record available at https://lccn.loc.gov/2022042779

Contents

Acknowledgments

The research and practice presented in this book rest heavily upon a particular notion of human development and of how we come to know the world of which we are a part. Because I believe that we can never fully know the reality of the world with which our enterprise collides, I recognize that the truth as presented in this writing is my truth, informed by my experience, by the meaning I have made of it, and for which I alone am responsible.

Because that truth has been shaped within the social world of my experience with others, I also acknowledge that nothing I have offered here would have been possible without their participation. It is in this context that I acknowledge the assistance of those students, colleagues, mentors, co-authors, and anonymous clients who made inestimable contributions to the ongoing dialogue that shaped the theory underlying, and drove the practice that informs, this work.

In particular, I acknowledge the substantive contributions to this writing provided by colleagues, Carl Glickman and John Dagley, with whom I have been fortunate to collaborate in testing these ideas and who encouraged my longstanding interest in putting these ideas to print. Of course, the book you hold would not have been realized without the critical and affirming critique of an anonymous reviewer. I would also like to acknowledge the support of those at Lexington Books, who helped in its production, especially Judith Lakamper and Mark Lopez whose enthusiasm and professionalism made this work possible.

Significantly, this book and the 40 years of teaching, scholarship, and clinical practice that it represents owe their existence to Bree A. Hayes. Without her sustained interest as a critical reviewer and persistent enthusiasm as an empowering colleague and spouse, this book would simply never have seen its final form. As well, I want to thank my children (Jon, Ali, Jessica, and Gillian) for their patience as unwitting participants in my efforts to test theory against the reality of their childhoods.

Finally, it should be acknowledged that material that I have published previously serves as the substrate for portions of the narrative and the presentation of key ideas that inform the discussion throughout this book. Although some passages are repeated verbatim, it would be fair to say that the entire text is informed by but does not replicate this work. Specific publications, all of which have been revised, excerpted, and/or adapted with the permission of their respective publishers are noted at the end of the respective chapters to which they contribute substantially, but not exclusively, and include:

Hayes, R. L. (1981). High school graduation: The case for identity loss. *Personnel and Guidance Journal, 59*, 369–371. Republished with permission of the American Counseling Association conveyed through Copyright Clearance Center, Inc.

Hayes, R. L. (1984). Coping with loss: A developmental approach to helping children and youth. *Counseling and Human Development, 17*(3), 1–12. Love Publishing, the rightsholder on record for this title, has ceased operation. Current rightsholder is unknown despite best efforts to identify.

Hayes, R. L. (1985). A primer of human development for counselors. *Journal of Humanistic Education and Development, 24*, 5–15. Republished with permission of the American Counseling Association conveyed through Copyright Clearance Center, Inc.

Hayes, R. L. (1986). Human growth and development. In M. Lewis, R. L. Hayes, & J. Lewis (Eds.), *An introduction to the counseling profession* (pp. 36–95). Itasca, IL: F. E. Peacock. Republished with permission of the author.

Hayes, R. L. (1991). Counseling and clinical implications of Kohlberg's developmental psychology. In L. Kuhmerker, U. Gielen, & R. L. Hayes (Eds.), *The Kohlberg legacy for the helping professions* (pp. 173–187). Birmingham, AL: Religious Education Press. Republished with permission of Religious Education Press.

Hayes, R. L. (1991). Applications of interactionist developmental schemes to counseling theory and practice. In L. Kuhmerker, U. Gielen, & R. L. Hayes (Eds.), *The Kohlberg legacy for the helping professions* (pp. 188–200). Birmingham, AL: Religious Education Press. Republished with permission of Religious Education Press.

Hayes, R. L. (1994). The legacy of Lawrence Kohlberg: Implications for counseling and human development. *Journal of Counseling and Development, 72*, 261–267. Republished with permission of the American Counseling Association conveyed through Copyright Clearance Center, Inc.

Hayes, R. L. (1994). Counseling in the postmodern world: Origins and implications of a constructivist developmental approach. *Counseling and Human Development, 26*(6), 1–12. Love Publishing, the rightsholder on record for this title, has ceased operation. Current rightsholder is unknown despite best efforts to identify.

Hayes, R. L., & Oppenheim, R. (1997). Constructivism: Reality is what you make it. In T. Sexton and B. Griffin, *Constructivist thinking in counseling practice, research, and training* (pp. 19–40). New York: Teachers College Press. Copyright 1997 by Teachers College, Columbia University. Republished with permission of the publisher. All rights reserved.

Hayes, R. L. (2001). Making meaning in groups: A constructivist developmental approach. In K. Fall & J. Levitov (Eds.), *Modern applications to group work* (pp. 263–280). Huntington, NY: Nova Science. Republished with permission of Nova Science Publishers, Inc.

Introduction

The first article I ever published was about loss, more than forty years ago (Hayes, 1981). Two years later, I was invited to write an article for counselors on helping children and youth to cope with loss from a developmental perspective (Hayes, 1984). It became the most requested single publication of its publisher. Since then, I published articles on related topics, gave lectures to and conducted workshops for audiences large and small, and taught a course on the subject. I even had a book contract at one point. But somehow, I always became distracted by some event, or circumstance, or what I imagined to be the magnitude of the project—until now.

Perhaps it's the search for purpose that comes with retirement. Or maybe it's the "leisure" time afforded by two years of social isolation during a pandemic. Or maybe it's the encouragement I got from an anonymous reviewer of a chapter I'd published recently on loss. Or maybe it's the persistent encouragement I got from my wife to finally bring this project to completion. And perhaps, as I complete the eighth decade of my life, it just may be time to put my thoughts on loss to print before they and I are lost as well.

Quite naturally, people often ask me how I got interested in "such a, well . . . , such a deadly topic. It's got to be pretty depressing." And then they end with the question, "Isn't it?" Actually, I find it deeply rewarding to write and speak about loss; I enjoy helping others talk about and understand their own losses. To understand my enjoyment, however, is to understand the point of this book. I believe that people are never more purely themselves than when they lose.

I met my wife's family for the first time at the funeral of her mother. In those first encounters, I was able to see a family love and care for one another without shame or embarrassment or the usual nervous rituals that accompany the introduction of a potential in-law. It might have taken me years to discover the real strengths and the attendant vulnerabilities in each of these people. But there they were for all to see. Her father apologized for not being able to be more attentive to me during his grief; her brother thanked me for helping organize things around the house during their mourning. When I told him "It wasn't anything anyone wouldn't have done," he replied firmly, "Perhaps, but it was you who did it."

In such moments, the basic character of each of these people was revealed: Harvey, the ever-attentive, supportive, mediating father who deals with his own losses by caring for the needs of others. And Marshall, the strong and silent big brother whose few carefully-chosen words always come straight from the heart. I met other family members, too, whom I've come to meet again and again over the years. With each meeting I am newly aware of how well I know each of them beneath the public masks they now wear.

I guess I've always been interested in loss and especially in its meaning for the loser. I am one of those lucky people who has a twin. Being a twin is a rather happy circumstance, although I didn't always think so. It allows a person to conduct one of life's great experiments. Nearly everyone has wondered what life would have been like "if only." Being a twin places you in this situation, whether you like it or not. As fraternal twins, the comparison took on the added dimension that we could not only compare hair color, eye color, height, weight, shoe size, and so on, but also life circumstances, athletic achievements, report cards, food preferences, friendships, and the like. My twin and I have found the list nearly inexhaustible. Having a twin let me see how my life might have turned out differently.

I was introduced to the formal study of loss in college. A course in medical sociology introduced me to the ground-breaking work of psychiatrist Elisabeth Kubler-Ross (1969) on death and dying. Breaking with the tradition of her time, she had the original idea to ask terminally-ill patients to teach physicians what they knew about dying. As someone trained in biology, I found myself an heir to the modernist's faith in the capacity of the individual to know, to understand, and to control nature as part of a grand plan to liberate the individual. Subsequent study in biology, systems theory, group dynamics, and developmental psychology began to erode that faith in a knowable universe. Further study brought me recurrently to the realization of how powerfully our experience of loss contributes to the person we have—and continue to—become. I also came to realize that not all share, nor have they ever, in this unifying narrative—a story we tell ourselves to explain ourselves to others and to ourselves. I've come to accept myself as a skeptic. As such, I believe we can never really know the truth of what happens because it is always being presented in the present within the context of the present. I have come instead to understand that truth lies in the collected truths (i.e., inter-subjectivity) we bring to understanding the world of our varied experiences. In effect, we cut a deal with one another, however tentatively, to accept the world as socially constructed.

Graduate study in counseling introduced me to the writings of Baldwin (1902/1897), Cooley (1902), Dewey (1897), James (1890), Kohlberg (1969), Mead (1934), Piaget (1954/1936), and Werner (1957) and to a set of ideas we now recognize as constructivism (Hayes, 2020). This system-oriented paradigm offers a dialectical synthesis of the false dichotomy of organism and environment. Constructivists believe that people are active and that the basic mental structures are reorganized and redefined through exercise and confrontation by opposing ideas. The process of knowing emerges from our attempts to make sense of our experiences within ourselves and the world in which we live. In this view, reality is constructed from experience and represents a relationship between the self and the world.

Constructivism asserts the following: (1) Humans operate as self-organizing meaning-making systems that attempt to make sense of their experience within themselves and the world; (2) Cognition is a process of relating events in a way that knowledge results from the interaction of organismic structuring tendencies and the structure of the outside world; (3) Human development is fundamentally a social process that emerges from transactions between ourselves and our personal surroundings; (4) Development is the natural outcome of successively more complex attempts to make meaning of our social experience; (5) Problems arise from limitations in current ways of knowing; and (6) Language provides a symbol system for grounding self-understanding in relation to others.

In sum, what one knows (or rather, how one is knowing it) emerges from interactions between organismic structuring tendencies and the structure of the outside world. Thus, reality is constructed from experience and represents a relationship between the self and the world. Each claim to know the truth is itself subject to comparison with yet another claim. As a result, we never get to see the constraints of the world with which our enterprise collides. Instead, what we experience, and thus come to know, is necessarily built up of our own building blocks. We don't discover reality as something out there or hidden within ourselves; rather, we invent it. In this sense, reality is what you make it.

As a counseling psychologist, I have been impressed with the regularity with which my clients' efforts at meaning-making are tied to their experiences of loss. Similarly, I find that when I share in their attempts to understand what is happening to them—to make sense of the loss—I gain a greater understanding of them as well. In the process of counseling, I routinely ask clients to consider what they have lost, emphasizing their experience rather than the object. In listening to their answers to my question "What did YOU lose?" I come to understand them more fully. I find I appreciate their struggle more deeply than I might in asking any other question. The meaning we make of loss is critically important to our growing sense of self in relation to others and to our efforts to construct a self that can be sustained in the face of recurring change.

This book is about how change brings loss to our lives, how we make meaning of that loss, and how our experience with loss directs our encounters with loss in the future. Each loss challenges us in this way: to rethink our worldview, to ask whom we have become, and to reinvent ourselves anew. Some losses are predictable, such as when relatives leave after a visit, or when grandparents die after a long illness. But many come as a surprise, especially to the minds of children whose years of experience are as limited as the sense they make of such events. Toys that break, stores that are closed, and friends who don't call are as mysterious to the minds of children, when first encountered, as premature death, divorce, and company-ordered moves are to the minds of adults. Each loss challenges us to rethink our worldview and to learn from it or be lost ourselves.

Central to understanding this process is understanding how we make meaning of loss and how that process is transformed over a lifetime. It is not so much about loss as it is about losing. And it is not so much about losing as it is about who we are when we lose. It is in these private moments of confronting our loss that we must confront ourselves in the loss. Because we only lose what is important to us, in the process, we discover what that importance is. Most especially, this book is about how we make meaning of loss in each period of our lives and how the way in which we meet each challenge directs our encounters with loss in the future.

This book is intended for people who want to know more about how we make meaning of loss and how that meaning is transformed over a lifetime. Taking a lifespan approach, this book serves as a guide to understanding how caregivers can help others in making better sense of their experience of loss. It is a guide not a recipe book. It tells you where to look, not what to see. It is meant to raise more questions than it answers and to provide answers only to point the way to further exploration.

This book is about how we can help others, especially children and adolescents, to learn from the losses in their lives. It is about how caregivers can identify the living vestiges of losses encountered in childhood that live on in the lives of adults. Suggestions are provided for how these earlier losses can become fruitful allies in encounters with change in the present. It is also about how adults may restructure their relationships in the present to transcend painful losses experienced as children in realizing a more reliable vision for the future.

There is a rich literature on death and death education (see Balk, 2014; Goldman, 2013; Kubler-Ross & Kessler, 2014; National Association of School Psychologists, 2015; Stroebe et al., 2008; Stillion & Attig, 2015; Szabo, 2009; Wheat & Whiting, 2018; Winokuer & Harris, 2016) and I've made no attempt to improve upon it here. Instead, my focus is less on death per se than on those little deaths that confront each of us in the enterprise of being human. In particular, the discussion is organized around three related areas: (1) loss as a part of life; (2) loss as a cumulative experience; and (3) mediating in the experience of loss.

Finally, this book is intended to be read by persons I refer to as "caregivers." By this term I mean those persons who are called upon by role, professional preparation, or personal interest to care for others, especially in times of grief and loss. Throughout, I have used this term, where appropriate, to refer to people such as counselors, psychologists, social workers, psychiatrists, clergy, physicians, nurses, teachers, coaches, school administrators, parents, custodians, and the like. I have chosen the term caregiver, rather than caretaker, deliberately to highlight the importance attached to caring as an activity that goes on between people. As developmental psychologist Carol Gilligan (1982) has noted:

> The experiences of inequality and interconnection, inherent in the relation of parent and child, then give rise to the ethics of justice and care, the ideals of human relationship—the vision that self and other will be treated as of equal worth, that despite differences in power, things will be fair; the vision that everyone will be responded to and included, that no-one will be left alone or hurt. (pp. 62–63)

Viewed in this way, caring is a way of relating such that the needs of the other are seen as inseparable from the needs of the self. In giving care to others, therefore, we care for ourselves as well. What could be fairer or more just than to treat another as one would treat oneself? Suggestions are provided throughout the book for how adults can help children and youth make meaning of the losses in their lives. Carrying these lessons forward into adulthood, caregivers can view how a lifetime of experience with loss creates the self-narrative that tells the story of a life past as much as it shapes the form of a life ahead. In the spirit of giving care, adult readers are likely to find these suggestions helpful guides as well in working through previous losses that live on inside the child within each of us.

LOOKING AHEAD

In this introduction, I've offered a view of humans as self-organizing systems engaged in complex, recursive transactions with others in a social environment. Through this self-constructive process, we are constantly engaged in making meaning of our experience. Meanings comprise the cognitive categories that make up a person's view of reality, that give direction to future action, and that structure the interpretation and application of knowledge. Because individuals construct their own reality in attempts to understand the world of their experience, the best we can hope for in understanding one another is a reliable, rather than a verifiable, road map to guide our future interactions. Understood in this way, learning results from organizing the meanings we make of our experience in the world. As we learn, meaning-making either reaffirms existing beliefs or provides the opportunity to create new meanings. Such is the experience of loss: to hold on to our notions of the world as we have known it up to this point or take the risk let go and entertain a new future yet unrealized. Such is the hope, as well, of any client who comes to counseling: to be understood and to find new meaning to direct future action. In the pages to follow, I explore how the process of meaning-making is central to our understanding of the relationship between loss and identity development. In doing so, I provide a guide to understanding the role meaning-making plays in how we come to know and how caregivers can help transform their experiences of loss over the lifespan.

Chapter 1: Loss as Part of Life introduces the idea that loss is not something that happens to us as we live but is living itself. Rather than a static event, each loss sets a cycle of change in motion that make our lives forever different than they might otherwise have been. It is our effort to make sense of loss (i.e., meaning-making) and the search for significance to be found in the products of this process (i.e., meanings made) that structure grieving.

Chapter 2: Making Meaning of Loss is about how change brings loss to our lives. As meaning-makers, we are embedded in a continuous process of negotiation and renegotiation of who we are and who we are in relation to others. And at each juncture in these negotiations, we are faced with calculating the cost of losing who we are (i.e., the self that has served us to this point) and acknowledging that who I've been is no longer who I'm about to become.

Chapter 3: Mediating in Loss applies a constructivist lens to reconceptualizing counseling as a means to reconstruct one's past understanding and rehearse alternative futures. In helping others transcend loss, caregivers should focus on how meaning is made in that space between a loss and the person's experience. How caregivers can promote this self-reflection by others as well as themselves provides a useful guide for mediating in loss.

Chapter 4: Infants and Toddlers, chapter 5: Middle Childhood, and chapter 6: Adolescents and Youth chronicle the development of the human capacity to make meaning of experience over the period from birth to roughly age 25–30. As we age, our experience with loss expands and with it come advances in the range and variability of coping strategies available for problem solving. These chapters explore the emergence of these capacities, the conditions promoting their development, and the unique ways in which loss is understood in each period.

Chapter 7: Midlife and chapter 8: Late(r) Life explore how the meanings made by adults over decades of experience with loss have been organized in an assumptive world of all that we believe to be true. Understanding how these assumptions shape our self-narratives, how caregivers can access these personal stories in understanding the other, and how reflecting on one's past behavior through life review can help in making meaning of a life well-lived complete these chapters.

Chapter 9: Caring for the Caregiver is set against the backdrop of a global pandemic that created losses so extensive, so arbitrary, so ambiguous, and so immediate as to defy every effort to construct a sustainable understanding of the world and our place in it. In a world where the pandemic has made experience a poor guide for future action, stress has overwhelmed our capacity for making meaning. This chapter illuminates the realities of dealing with ambiguous loss during the pandemic as seen through the experiences of three caregivers: a restaurateur, a nurse, and a teacher. Recognizing that you can't be much help to others if you don't take care of yourself first, the remainder of this chapter explores what caregivers can do to care for themselves.

NOTE

Adapted from R. L. Hayes (1994). Counseling in the postmodern world: Origins and implications of a constructivist developmental approach. *Counseling and Human Development, 26*(6), 1–12. Love Publishing, the rightsholder on record for this title, has ceased operation. Current rightsholder is unknown despite best efforts to identify; R. L. Hayes. (2020). *Making meaning: A constructivist approach to counseling and groupwork in education.* Washington, DC: Lexington/Rowman & Littlefield. Republished with permission of Lexington/Rowman & Littlefield; R. L. Hayes, & R. Oppenheim. (1997). Constructivism: Reality is what you make it. In T. Sexton and B. Griffin: *Constructivist Thinking in Counseling Practice, Research, and Training* (pp. 19–40). New York: Teachers College Press. Copyright 1997 by Teachers College, Columbia University. Republished with permission of the publisher. All rights reserved.

Chapter 1

Loss as Part of Life

Loss is not something that happens to us as we live; it is living itself. Each loss challenges the illusion of our omnipotence and threatens to destroy our very being. In working through rather than around each loss, we take the risk to build a more competent self—a self that can make better sense of the world we're part of. Understood in this way, human development represents the course of our attempts to make sense of the changes going on around us. How we understand each loss is part of an ongoing evolution in how we make meaning itself. As a meaning-making system, the self undergoes regular and predictable changes. By these changes, former losses are resolved and the possibility of experiencing new ones is created. How we think about loss, in particular, is influenced by how we think, in general. Understanding how our thinking changes over a lifetime provides a valuable framework to study loss and our reactions to it. But first, a bit of autobiography to set the stage.

Eight was a very special age for me. I got a new bicycle. Nearly four years had passed—half a lifetime—since my new tricycle was stolen only two days after I got it. Then I watched, green with envy, as my twin rode his trike about. Oh, he was generous in letting me use it from time to time; but it was his, and mine was gone. I pleaded with my parents to get a new one, arguing that it "just wasn't fair." Yes, I had been asked to put my trike away. Yes, I had been advised that it might otherwise be damaged or even stolen. And yes, I had even been cautioned that it wouldn't be replaced. What I didn't know was that my dad didn't have the money to replace it, much as he had wanted to.

Now I had a bicycle. And every night I put it away. When it was scratched, I painted it. When it was broken, I fixed it. And when I was 15, I sold it. What friends that blue Columbia and I had been! But I was interested in cars now, "too old for just a bicycle." I said "goodbye" and "thanks" to the kid who bought it, and for just a moment I thought about saying the same to that bike as it and my childhood went rolling down the driveway together.

Life is a series of "goodbyes." Yet, like a doorway that marks the passage of our lives, loss presents the opportunity to say "hello" to new learning

1

experiences. The crises that form the context of our goodbyes are the natural consequence of living so as to preserve the present in the face of change. In each step forward in our evolution, we must necessarily leave something behind. With each loss there is the consequent loss of a part of our selves. And yet, through these losses we gain new opportunities to learn about the selves we are becoming. Thus, each crisis holds the possibility for our own transformation.

I learned a lot in those bicycle years. I learned to ask strangers for directions and how to sit next to them on a bus; I learned to talk with relatives who knew all about me but whom I had never met; I learned how to start a conversation with classmates who were new to school and I to theirs. I also learned that robins die when they fall from their nests; I learned to wait by myself when my mom was late in arriving home from work; I learned to be patient when shopping with my dad.

In the six decades since, I've learned a lot about what it means to lose, and the opportunity loss offers us to reinvent ourselves. I've learned that much of life is serendipitous—that living is more about having a purpose than a plan. What you do about any loss is as much about who'll you become as it is a measure of who you've been. And all of loss is set in this context: our history, current circumstances, and our vision for the future. Flush with the profits from a windfall sale, my dad was on his way home to celebrate this moment of success for his fledgling tool company. Impatient and still far from home, he bought two tricycles on impulse as he gassed up at a roadside station. As much as the loss of my trike was its own lesson in individual responsibility for me, it was a cautionary tale for my dad whose dreams would not be so easily realized. Successes would be temporary as would the pain of any failure. Loss and transcendence would become thematic as persistence overcame despair in each recalculation of his life's trajectory. As we'll see in the end, hope and determination would be his greatest allies.

LOSS AND LIFE

Advanced technology has made death the province of the hospital, while the natural life cycle of the farm is as remote an experience for most children as is a field trip to the museum to see animals that *once lived*. But today's children are not without loss. Approximately one in fourteen Americans are estimated to lose a sibling or parent before they reach age 18 (New York Life Foundation/National Alliance for Grieving Children, 2021). Add the losses associated with divorce, remarriage, incarceration, drug addiction, health-related issues, and domestic violence, and the extent to which loss affects the lives of young people becomes obvious.

EVERY DAY IN AMERICA

2 mothers die from complications of childbirth.
5 children are killed by abuse or neglect.
8 children or teens die by suicide.
9 children or teens are killed with a gun.
20 children or teens die from accidents.
46 children or teens are injured with a gun.
59 babies die before their first birthday.
121 children are arrested for violent crimes.
223 children are arrested for drug crimes.
514 public school students are corporally punished.*
678 babies are born without health insurance.
860 babies are born with low birth weight.
1,541 babies are born into poverty.
1,785 children are confirmed as abused or neglected.
1,909 children are arrested.
2,906 high school students drop out.*
14,206 public school students are suspended.*
*Based on 180 school days a year (Children's Defense Fund, 2021, p. 8).

Today's children are witnesses to mass shootings that occur with regularity in public spaces including schools, houses of worship, concert venues, shopping malls, community centers, nightclubs, and movie theaters. It's not surprising that a survey of students aged 15–19 found 75 percent reported mass shootings as a significant source of stress. Nearly as many (72 percent) reported the same about school shootings or the possibility of them occurring (American Psychological Association, 2018). In 2020 alone, there were 4,977 incidents of gun violence in the United States, which killed or injured 123,428 individuals, of whom 5,146 were under the age of 18 (Gun Violence Archive, 2021). Recognizing that 85 percent of children under 13 who were killed by a firearm were killed in their own homes (Center for Violence Prevention, 2021), today's children are coming to learn that there is no safe place.

Their fears aside, young people today are confronted daily with reminders of their vulnerability to death and disease. Witness the omnipresence of zombies "in global popular culture, from video games and top-rated cable shows in the United States to comic books and other visual art forms to low-budget films from Cuba and the Philippines" (Lauro, 2017). This preoccupation with the undead is sustained in the public consciousness by a 24-hour news cycle that brings us "news as it happens" on "everything you need to know." The war(s) on terrorism, debates over climate change, nuclear disarmament, gun control and rampage shootings, exclusion and oppression by race, gender and sexual orientation, and the latest statistics on a global pandemic are all on display. Advertisements provide the only interruptions as we learn of health-care products, exercise equipment, diet routines, and details on the latest drug treatment for a disease you didn't know you had, and the lengthy list of possible adverse side effects should you decide to accept the invitation to "call for your trial sample in the next ten minutes."

Selling fitness is a multi-billion-dollar industry in the United States today. It appeals to a recurring fear that the self may be overwhelmed at any moment by forces beyond our control. This is an old theme in Western civilization (Janoff-Bulman, 1997, p. 93), but its form now pervades American culture. Americans are at war with more than their own bodies, they are at war with life itself. Beyond the more than $725 billion budgeted on defense, Americans spend more than $14 billion on coffee, $80 billion on cigarettes, $240 billion on alcohol, and $3.3 trillion on health care annually (Bureau of Labor Statistics, 2019).

A global pandemic, increasing authoritarianism, health and wealth disparities, and polarization around a host of issues including gun rights, climate change, reproductive rights, and immigration offer up likely causes for what Americans fear most. I suggest these are consequences rather than causes occasioned by threats to what Americans value most. Few will disagree that the core value for most Americans is individualism. Its corollaries include independence, freedom, self-reliance, free enterprise, and a work ethic that professes you get out of life what you put into it. In turn, what lies at the heart of what Americans fear most is losing control. This fear is what literary critic Tony Tanner (1971) calls the "dread that someone else is patterning your life, that there are all sorts of invisible plots afoot to rob you of your autonomy of thought and action, that conditioning is ubiquitous" (p. 15). At the risk of being unnecessarily reductionistic, this analysis suggests a growing concern that negotiating one's place in an ever-changing and indeterminant world poses the recurrent possibility that one will lose control and one's self in the process.

Even if by some miracle we could prevent the big losses noted above, or if we could at least protect our children from them, how could we protect them from all of those other losses that so inevitably come their way: the loss of a pet through death; the loss of one's place in the family through the birth of a sibling; the loss of one's culture as the result of a change in the social order; the loss of older siblings through the natural progression of their leaving home; the loss of function through illness; the loss of self-esteem that can come with being bullied or failing in school; the loss of direction that comes when expectations are unmet; the loss of security that accompanies the loss of a treasured object; or the loss of one's innocence in choosing to grow up.

The question is not how to help children avoid the losses they might experience. Instead, we need to help them experience the loss, to get *through* instead of *over* it.

As Kubler-Ross (1969) argues cogently:

> It is the denial of death that is partially responsible for people living empty, purposeless lives; for when you live as if you'll live forever, it becomes too easy to postpone the things you know that you must do. In contrast, when you fully understand that each day you awaken could be the last you have, you take the time that day to grow, to become more of who you really are, to reach out to other human beings. . . . For only when we understand the real meaning of death to human existence will we have the courage to become what we are destined to be. (pp. 164–165)

LOSS AS A CUMULATIVE EXPERIENCE

Life holds predictable psychosocial crises for us over the course of our development. These crises do not pose a threat of catastrophe as much as they represent "crucial periods of increased vulnerability and heightened potential" (Erikson, 1968, p. 96). When worked out in a constructive manner, the resolution of these crises can result in a new balance of forces within the individual. Failure to negotiate the crisis limits our capacity for further development as seen in this excerpt from a letter by Goethe to a friend upon the death of his child:

> In such cases one does not know whether it is better to succumb to pain naturally or to pull oneself together with the assistance provided for us by culture. If one decides for the latter, as I always do, one is only better for a moment, and I have noted that nature demands its right through other crises. (cited in Spiegel, 1977, p. 91)

A reluctance to acknowledge the losses in one's life can place lasting constraints on the enjoyment of that life in the future. This is not to say that any loss once resolved won't also make further demands. Rather, it is our efforts to make sense of loss (i.e., meaning-making) and the search for significance to be found in the products of this process (i.e., meanings made) that structure grieving. As noted in the Introduction, I first became interested in the formal study of loss upon reading the work of Elisabeth Kubler-Ross. After interviewing some 500 terminally-ill patients, she outlined five stages in coming to terms with death: (1) denial (refusal to accept the reality of what is happening); (2) anger; (3) bargaining (especially for more time); (4) depression, and (5) acceptance of the inevitability of death.

Critics are quick to point out that Kubler-Ross' "stages" are not true stages in the sense that they describe a fixed sequence (Holland & Neimeyer, 2010; Neimeyer, 2001). The developmental course of grieving is not so much the linear progression of stages offered by Kubler-Ross (1969; Kubler-Ross & Kessler, 2014) and others (e.g., Bowlby, 1980; Marris, 1986; Parkes et al., 1996). It is a mix of thoughts and feelings as the loss is experienced again and anew in recursive efforts at understanding. Instead, it is better to think of them as a constellation of reactions through which a person may explore any loss. Indeed, I have seen many individuals go back and forth between anger and acceptance or show conflicting reactions such as denial and acceptance simultaneously. Grieving is less a set of stages or periods through which one travels, and more an ongoing process of finding a balance (however temporary) between the past and an emerging self. As C. S. Lewis (1964/1961) so poignantly described his own grieving process following the death of his wife: "For in grief nothing 'stays put.' One keeps on emerging from a phase, but it always recurs. Round and round. Everything repeats. Am I going in circles, or dare I hope I am on a spiral?" (p. 27).

As with living, dying is an individual experience for which there is no "best" way. The point is to recognize that people have understandable, if not entirely predictable, responses to the course of death. As I will argue, a similar process underlies our attempts to deal with losses of all kinds. The experience of loss is a journey of discovery, of consideration of what has been lost and of what is to be found along the way. Although a past loss may be resolved only to be experienced once again, it also presents an opportunity to rework past meanings and to experiment with a new self yet unrealized. As philosopher Thomas Attig (2011) explains: "losses transform the world as we experience it, sometimes pervasively. Coming to terms with the changes requires that we relearn the world. . . . [Doing so] is not a matter of *learning information about the world* but *learning how to be and act in the world* differently in the light of our loss (pp. 105, 107; emphases in original). Even if we accept the loss, a return to intense grief can be triggered by many things. These events include holidays, something we see or hear, taste or smell, recovering a lost keepsake, the death of pet or close relative, along with developmental issues, especially for children. Knowing that the sense of loss can come around again helps us to be prepared for the experience and perhaps to envision better more satisfying resolutions to the loss in our efforts to relearn the world we now inhabit.

Jean had come to me initially seeking help resolving some anxiety issues she attributed to her new status as someone recently divorced. In the course of our work together, she related a story of having suddenly burst into tears at the wedding of her nephew at the moment he said, "I do." Perplexed by her reaction to "what was supposed to be a very happy event," she described feeling increasingly "resentful, and then hurt, and finally a deep sense of loss. And then I lost it." In what I have found to be the most important question to ask under such circumstances, I said: "What did you lose?" When asking this question, I particularly like to stress the word "you" rather than "what" to focus clients on their experience rather than on the lost object. After several false starts, Jean became more focused on her own loss in the moment—not of crying, or a loss of control, but of her infant son some two decades earlier. "I thought I was over that by now. I thought I'd put his death to rest," she lamented. "I suspect you have," I suggested. "But this loss is new. It's not his death you mourn now but rather the reality of his marriage, of your happiness in the moment, and of the realization that this too will never happen. It's a loss you might have expected but couldn't experience, at least until now."

Jean, like many people, believed that loss was something that happens to you, you deal with it, and it goes away. Each loss is not only born of change, but it creates change, which creates new losses in turn. Rather than a static event, each loss sets a cycle of change in motion that make our lives forever different than they might have been. Having encountered and even transcended one loss, we encounter other, associated losses that challenge us anew. Take the simple case of losing your car keys. There is, of course, the time lost in searching for them, the potential cost of replacing them, the opportunities lost in not finding them in time, and the energy expended in searching your mind as well as the local environment to find them. The loss, however temporary, opens opportunities to examine the importance of what's been missed, to review the value in seeking help from others, or to realize the limits of our control. Depending upon how often this scenario plays itself out in our lives, we may resolve to adopt new precautionary behaviors. Hiding a spare set of keys, enlisting the help of others, or simply admitting that "stuff happens" offer possibilities for managing loss in a future yet to be encountered.

As will be elaborated in chapter 2, human development represents the course of our attempts to make sense of the changes going on around us and, with each change, to experience a set of associated losses. With each developmental advance, people process their life experiences in more complex ways. In so doing they often relive the events of a prior loss as new circumstances pose the reality of losses yet unexperienced. This resurgence of grief can mean living and reliving the events of a prior loss as new circumstances bring us face to face with new losses. As Neubert (2009) reflects, "life remains perilous, no matter how elaborated and sophisticated our symbolic systems of prediction and control may be" (p. 175). Just as Jean could not have fully experienced the loss of her son's now imagined wedding, the reality of future divorces, births, funerals, anniversaries, reunions, relocations, hirings, firings, and retirements all provide fresh opportunities to explore the meaning in each loss and *what it means to be me at a time like this under circumstances like these.*

CHANGE, LOSS, AND PAIN

Don't it always seem to go / That you don't know

what you've got / 'Til it's gone. (Mitchell, 1970)

Have you ever noticed how you can fall asleep in a crowded room and yet awake suddenly in front of your computer, in the dark, as the monitor times out in sleep mode? Have you ever noticed you can see lint easier on a plain suit than on a plaid one? Have you ever noticed how much easier it is to criticize than to praise someone, especially if you have high hopes for them? Of course, you've noticed, but have you ever wondered why?

Humans are hard-wired to recognize patterns. Rather than re-calculate the details of one's life daily, we learn to attend to the different, the novel, the surprising. Assuming that what hasn't killed us already won't harm us, we engage in a kind of evolutionary strategy by monitoring change to identify only what is different. Fundamentally, habits are born in this way: starting the day on the "right" side of the bed; going through your "morning routine"; joking that you've taken the same path to work so often that "the car knows the way." And yet, how often have you gotten out of bed in a hotel and bumped the wall or stumbled over a chair unexpectedly? Or had your "morning routine" interrupted by a lack of hot water, toothpaste, or a "misplaced" bar of soap? Or found yourself on your routine path to work only to realize that wasn't where you intended to go that day?

The nervous system is designed to tell us what's different. It analyzes change. So it is that we cannot smell ourselves, or after a time, our own fragrance, or the fish we may be cooking. But when others enter the room, they may immediately take notice of these scents. What we have long since failed to notice in its presence, others now recognize as a change in their own environments. This system has a simple logic: it acts to protect us against the possibility of harm. So it is that change—every change—poses the possibility of our own death (figuratively, if not literally).

Of course, life without change is its own form of death. Nonetheless, change must occur within certain limits if we are to respond to it most effectively—not so large that it overwhelms us and not so small that we don't notice—leaving us somewhere between fear and boredom. Ironically, this balancing act means that individuals will necessarily need to change in order to remain the same. To maintain this homeostasis in a changing environment, all living things have evolved systems of responses to monitor change. By monitoring the changes that take place about us, we are ever alert to the dangerous and the fresh opportunities that can exist for us. As humans, we undertake various physical and mental responses to these challenges, which we experience as stress. These stress responses are generally positive and help us to prepare for danger by keeping us alert, motivated, or protected from bodily harm. In response to acute stress, for example, the body's sympathetic nervous system is activated by the sudden release of hormones. These hormones trigger the release of yet other hormones. And these hormones, in turn, initiate a chain of reactions that increase heart rate, raise blood pressure, dilate pupils, and elevate breathing all to prepare the body for "fight or flight." Our heightened attention when preparing for an exam, our excitement at going on vacation, sneezing when suddenly struck by sunshine, or the anxiety we feel at meeting new people are all examples of these positive stress responses.

Because culture helps to shape what people value, members of different cultures vary in the types of stressors they're exposed to. The significance of any stressor and responses to it are shaped by cultural conditions. For example, in parts of the world where natural disasters such as earthquakes or tornadoes are more common, exposure to extreme stressors is more likely. Likewise, different sources of stress are experienced by members of a minority culture living within a majority culture. For example, immigrant refugees newly arrived in their host countries face greater rates of discrimination and threats of job loss (Schwartz et al., 2018). As well, persons from collectivist cultures, such as Chinese, are more likely to seek social support and maintain community harmony when stressed. By contrast, persons from individualistic cultures, such as Americans, who value independence and individual responsibility, are more likely to feel stressed when their autonomy is being threatened (Luong et al., 2020). As exemplified, culture provides a context for making meaning of stressful events as part of a highly complex, continually changing system of meanings that is learned, shared, transmitted, and altered from one generation to another (Triandis, 2001). While culture contributes significantly to what meaning is made and what actions are taken, it is the universal process of meaning-making that is central to understanding the relationship between loss and stress.

By the very recognition of change, we must acknowledge the loss of a way of being that was, to this point at least, self-sustaining. More precisely, in losing we recognize the object of our loss; that is, we are forced to know it again. In the process, we come to know ourselves again as well. When a treasured object is misplaced, it is not until we look for it and fail to find it that it is "lost" *for us*. Or were a close friend to die as you read this passage, you wouldn't experience the loss until you were notified of the death. Yet in becoming aware of the death, you would likely be aware of only selected aspects of the loss. Perhaps you would think of your friend's family, or of vacations you'd never take together, or of the laughter you'd never share. The point to be made here is that in losing, it is our coming to know the loss that is central to our experience of the loss.

When we lose, our identities, the selves we have chosen to become and to which we have been committed, go out of balance. Because change is constant, every change will necessarily be accompanied by the experience of loss. Most, but not all, such perturbations will lead to necessary structural changes that preserve the system. The pain that we experience when we lose is the system's way of telling us that something has gone "wrong." In this way, our emotions may be seen as arising out of this experience of coming to know. Rather than view cognition and affect as antagonists, think of them as partners; two forms arising from the same basic structure, which finds itself under attack. Think of your emotions as a kind of affective barometer that measures the rise and fall in intensity of various threats to your self-system. In such a system, pain acts as a kind of smoke alarm—a call to action that alerts us to the need to do something to achieve a new balance for a system that has somehow been set in motion.

> Pain is about the resistance to the motion of life. Our attempt to deny what has happened and is happening causes pain. . . . In defense against the losses which have already occurred, in defense against the experience of grief and mourning, we inflict on ourselves a pain which is greater than the loss itself. Grieving and mourning are not really painful; they are our reunion with life itself and our recognition of its motion. Anxiety and melancholia, which set us against life, are a greater source of pain than life itself, however much, change must always have to do with loss. (Kegan, 1982, pp. 265–266)

Critically, it isn't *change* that people resist; it's *loss*. Indeed, most people are quite optimistic about change, routinely seeking out "the new and improved." But they are less sanguine about the potential losses that may accompany giving up control over that future. Given the developmental inevitably of recurring loss, the question is not how to avoid the losses we experience but, rather, how to experience the loss and make sense of it.

> Seven-year-old Stefon was brought to the counselor's office by his teacher after arriving at school crying uncontrollably. The boy explained that his sister had recently been killed in a car accident. Puzzled that Stefon had been sent to school, the counselor called his home. After answering the phone, his mother explained that she felt it was best to send her son to school to get his mind off the death of his gerbil that had been found dead in its cage that morning.
>
> It was his pet that had been killed, not his sister; in fact, he didn't even have a sister! As the mother listened, the counselor emphasized that her son

experienced a deep sense of loss accompanied by feelings of sadness and confusion. Apparently unable to garner any support for his grief over the loss of a gerbil, he felt helpless, confused, and misunderstood. He rightly assumed that in order to legitimize his pain and sadness, he had to make up a story "worthy" of his grief. He could not stop crying until someone listened and allowed him to express his own feelings of loss and sadness, even for his pet.

It's the size of the "person" not the size of the "event" that determines the size of the "loss." By this statement, person is meant to refer to the system of meanings, of fundamental assumptions that form the core identity of the person. It is here that the event is transformed through meaning-making from something that happened to the person to become an experience for the person. Understood in this way, loss and the emotions that accompany it are the felt experience of the failure of our presumptive assumptions to preserve our identities in the face of change. The selves we have chosen to become and to which we are now committed are out of balance. Because we live in a dynamic environment of ever-changing conditions, we must necessarily make modifications *in anticipation of* desired outcomes that will preserve our unity in the face of such demands. The anticipation of continued or enduring pain, however, can lead to suffering and to chronic stress. As can be seen in figure 1.1, change, loss, and pain are linked by a sequence of self-regulated autopoietic events.

Rather than acknowledge the loss and our lack of control over it, we defend ourselves against that reality by trying to manage the loss instead. Drawing upon the original work in stages of grief noted above, Davenport (1981) proposed a list of assumptions that seem to underlie the emotions commonly associated with loss:

> Denial: This couldn't possibly happen to me without my permission!; Anger: How dare this happen? It's not fair and I won't allow it!; Bargaining: The only circumstances under which I'll go along with this are . . . ; Depression: I'm not worth much if this could happen. I must have some irremediable inadequacy that caused this; Panic: My psychological survival depends on keeping this loss from occurring; Worry: If I plan things carefully enough, I can at least make sure nothing makes me feel this vulnerable again. (p. 333)

A certain arrogance runs through these assumptions that we can somehow be more than human in the face of loss, that we can overcome it by insisting that losses of all kinds obey us. As such, our reactions to loss can best be understood as the result of trying to maintain our illusions of omnipotence in the face of a lack of control. Although pain is a natural consequence of loss, our efforts to control the loss can lead to suffering. This prolonged emotional response often supplants the original experience of loss. Carried beyond a

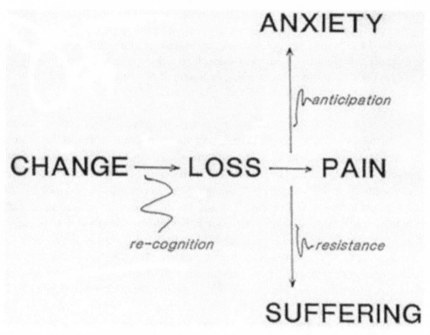

Figure 1.1. The Relationship Between Change, Loss, and Pain *Source:* Adapted from R. L. Hayes (1984), Coping with loss: A developmental approach to helping children and youth, *Counseling and Human Development, 17*(3), 1–12. Love Publishing, the rightsholder on record for this title, has ceased operation. Current rightsholder is unknown despite best efforts to identify.

response to the original pain, suffering involves a certain nurturance and cultivation of the pain. Seen in this way, suffering can be used to justify the loss and to demonstrate one's power over it. In the extreme, suffering can be elevated to an art form seen in the example of the mother who'd rather read in the dark than trouble her children to turn on a light. Children, too, learn quickly how responsive adults can be to their losses. I imagine that many an acting career was launched in a child's personal reactions to loss in the presence of one's family.

Similarly, the anticipation of future losses and the consequent pain and potential suffering can lead to chronic stress. In the latest of its annual polls on stress, the American Psychological Association (2021) found that 84 percent of adults reported feeling at least one emotion associated with prolonged stress in the prior two weeks. The most common of which were feelings of anxiety (47 percent), sadness (44 percent) and anger (39 percent). The majority of adults reported that the future of our nation (81 percent), the coronavirus pandemic (80 percent), and political unrest around the country (74 percent) were significant sources of stress in their lives. Beyond the serious health problems, such as heart disease, high blood pressure, diabetes, and other illnesses that arise from persistent strain on the body, the significant mental health issues that accompany prolonged stress have made anxiety disorders the most common mental illness in the United States, affecting one of every five Americans (World Health Organization, 2017).

Change and stressors have a major influence on mood, our sense of well-being, behavior, and health. Acute stress responses in young, healthy individuals may be adaptive and typically do not impose a health burden. However, if the threat is unremitting, particularly in older or unhealthy individuals, the long-term effects of stressors can damage health. The relationship between psychosocial stressors and disease is affected by the nature, number, and persistence of the stressors as well as by the individual's biological vulnerability (i.e., genetics, constitutional factors), psychosocial resources, and learned patterns of coping. Psychosocial interventions have proven useful for treating stress-related disorders and may influence the course of chronic diseases.

CHANGE AND CHOICE

If we can accept that change is constant, if not also entirely predictable, we are faced with a far more startling realization. With every change there is the accompanying experience of loss. Essentially, it is one's self that loses and, more importantly, it is one's self that is lost. If change is constant, loss and pain are inevitable. But suffering—especially the sort that accompanies chronic stress—is optional. Although we must be responsive as living organisms to change, we nonetheless have some options in the choices we make. These choices are at the core of what it means to be a human *being*. As the philosopher John Dewey (1960/1932) argued:

> In committing oneself to a particular course, a person gives a lasting set to his own being. Consequently, it is proper to say that in choosing this subject, rather than that, one is in reality choosing what kind of a person or self one is going to be. The self reveals its nature in what it chooses. (pp. 148–151)

Just as our choices reveal the kind of self we would like to be, so they reveal the kind of self we have been. In the course of our evolution toward a new self, each choice represents an opportunity to speculate on a future self and represents the danger in giving up a familiar past.

> Tony is a very successful, thirty-two-year-old bank executive with a newly awarded advanced degree, a new position, and a new home. He had come to me

originally seeking help with building a more effective relationship with his wife while adjusting to what he referred to as "lifestyle inflation." In time, the differences between their levels of satisfaction with the changes brought on by his recent successes revealed a gap between their basic values that proved too great to be bridged by their marriage, at least in its present form. He acknowledged that working hard had been the means to earning the kind of home and professional respect he "would like to have some day." Now that someday had arrived, he had lost his purpose for the struggle and was beginning to question the values that underlay the choices made so far. Wanting to be happy, he nonetheless was feeling trapped by the perceived conflict between the obligations of his marriage and his employer. The resulting moral impasse had left him feeling angry at the injustice and depressed by the loss of a dream. Faced with the necessity to change their relationship, and himself in the process, he wondered "Why didn't I see this coming? Why hadn't I been prepared? How could I be so successful in my professional life and such a failure in my personal life?"

The questions were not new to me. Clients often ask these things as they come face to face with their responsibility for past choices, especially those made in childhood. "Growing up poor and living in public housing, all I thought I ever wanted was to get a good job and be able to own my own home. So how come it all seems so hollow now?" Yet there was a question beneath Tony's questions. I asked: "Maybe you're also asking yourself how can I know for certain that I won't make the same mistakes, or worse, in the future?"

And in a telling response he replied: "Yes, that's it exactly. And I wonder do I really have the courage to go on—to try and maybe make new mistakes—or shouldn't I just keep the life I have and live with mistakes I know and can at least understand. I've lost so much already. I don't know if I can or want to lose any more." "And if you don't take the risk to change?," I prompted. "Then," he sighed, "I might lose a better future instead."

You don't have to think back very far in your life to realize that change is ongoing. Consider the attack on New York's Twin Towers in 2001, or the Financial Crisis of 2007–2008, or the devastation wrought by multiple hurricanes (Sandy in 2012; Harvey, Irma, and Maria in 2017; Michael in 2018) in the following decade, or the attack on the nation's Capitol that ushered in the current decade on January 6, 2021. Pick any point in time in your recent past and ask yourself how many things have happened since that time that have surprised you. Now look an equal distance into the future and ask yourself how clearly you can foresee the events that lie ahead? In a world where the weather is forecast in percentages and political pollsters report different percentages on every imaginable issue with a "plus or minus 3–4% margin of error," it should not surprise you that the future will surprise you. The surprise we experience in the face of change is nothing more or less than a signal that something is somehow different from what we had expected. The problem lies not in noticing the difference but rather in what sense we make of the difference. In effect, does this difference make a difference? In its simplest form, are we confronted by peril or possibility?

It is one thing to understand oneself and know what you want to be. It is quite another thing to have the courage to be who you really want to be. Each loss challenges us in this way: to have the courage to work through the loss toward the kind of person we are to become. In the pages ahead, we will explore how we learn to live with loss. As well, we'll see how we can help those we care for to become their best selves in the face of the losses that can and will challenge them. In the process, we will come to understand how we make meaning of loss and how that understanding can help us to make the most of the opportunity each loss presents.

NOTE

Adapted from R. L. Hayes. (1985). A primer of human development for counselors. *Journal of Humanistic Education and Development, 24,* 5–15. Republished with permission of the American Counseling Association conveyed through Copyright Clearance Center, Inc.; R. L. Hayes. (1986). Human growth and development. In M. Lewis, R. L. Hayes, & J. Lewis (Eds.). *An introduction to the counseling profession* (pp. 36–95). Itasca, IL: F. E. Peacock. Republished with permission of the author; R. L. Hayes. (1991). Counseling and clinical implications of Kohlberg's developmental psychology. In L. Kuhmerker, U. Gielen, & R. L. Hayes (Eds.), *The Kohlberg legacy for the helping professions* (pp. 173–187). Birmingham, AL: Religious Education Press. Republished with permission of Religious Education Press; R. L. Hayes. (1994). The legacy of Lawrence Kohlberg: Implications for counseling and human development. *Journal of Counseling and Development, 72,* 261–267. Republished with permission of the American Counseling Association conveyed through Copyright Clearance Center, Inc.; R. L. Hayes. (2020). *Making meaning: A constructivist approach to counseling and groupwork in education.* Washington, DC: Lexington/Rowman & Littlefield. Republished with permission of Lexington/Rowman & Littlefield; R. L. Hayes, & R. Oppenheim. (1997). Constructivism: Reality is what you make it. In T. Sexton and B. Griffin, *Constructivist Thinking in Counseling Practice, Research, and Training* (pp. 19–40). New York: Teachers College Press. Copyright 1997 by Teachers College, Columbia University. Republished with permission of the publisher. All rights reserved.

Chapter 2

Making Meaning of Loss

As humans, we occupy a social world of changing perspectives. In that world, what is known is the product of our own efforts to make sense of our unique experience, especially with others. The inevitability of change, however, challenges our understanding of that world and gives rise to what we experience as loss. Thus, the meaning we make of loss is critically important to our efforts to construct a more stable understanding of the world that can be sustained in the face of recurrent change. Further, this development of greater understandings takes place within a social context that is itself changed by our interactions with others, especially caregivers. From this view, knowledge is established through meanings constructed through experience, especially with others.

Central to understanding the role loss plays in our lives is to accept the notion that individuals bring their own reality to addressing life's problems. Although each of us is different, knowing how humans develop can help us understand these differences within the context of a universal human process. As well, this knowledge helps us understand how we make meaning of the losses that accompany predictable as well as unexpected life changes. Understanding how we make meaning in our lives has profound implications for understanding our reactions to loss and the role experience with others plays in the promotion of human development.

MAKING MEANING AND MEANINGS MADE

Interest in meaning has generated an extensive body of research on meaning-making and on meanings made, especially related to stressful life events (Janoff-Bulman & Frantz, 1997; Neimeyer et al., 2010; Park, 2010). Despite the proliferation of approaches, research into the effect of cognitive processing of traumatic events shows a high degree of consensus on their basic tenets. These "common and important characteristics" include:

(a) Prior to traumatic events, people have mental schemas that contain information about themselves and their world;

(b) Recovery from trauma requires individuals to process the trauma-related information until it can be incorporated into pre-existing inner models or until it can be modified to accommodate the new information;

(c) Attempts to integrate the trauma into a schematic representation will be proportional to the extent to which they experience distress;

(d) Traumatic memories must be activated so that they can be integrated into schematic representations; and,

(e) Individuals whose pre-existing schemas can accommodate the information inherent in a traumatic event will adjust to the event more rapidly than individuals whose pre-existing schemas are discordant with the information inherent in the event. (Lepore et al., 1996, pp. 271–272)

This research has been critical to our understanding of how people make sense of loss (i.e., meaning-making) and of the products of meaning-making processes (i.e., meanings made). In particular, we need to distinguish between the search for comprehensibility and the search for significance. As Taylor (1983) explained:

> Meaning is exemplified by, but not exclusively determined by, the results of an attributional search that answers the question, "What caused the event to happen?" . . . Meaning is also reflected in the answer to the question, "What does my life mean now?" (p. 1161).

As presented in chapter 1, meaning-making is ongoing and the anxiety and suffering that accompany chronic stress are byproducts of efforts to make sense of any change. Critically, this statement means that distress does not initiate the meaning-making process. Instead, distress is a consequence of efforts to reconcile the difference between the world as known and the world as experienced in the moment. The central implication of this claim is that we do not see the world as it is "in reality." Rather, we see the world as we understand that world to be.

In our efforts to differentiate a world independent of our constructs from our understanding of that world, our notions of "reality" undergo constant revision. Therefore, it is critical to understand that loss is experienced in the moment of the event within the meaning-making system of the individual. Efforts to resolve the discrepancy can *then* lead to meanings made such as acceptance, changes in global beliefs, identity, causal understanding, or denial of the discrepancy or of its significance. Indeed, research on the role of meaning-making in adaptation to bereavement found that "sense-making emerged as the most robust predictor of adjustment to bereavement [while] benefit finding interacted with sense making, with the fewest complications predicted when participants reported high sense, but low personal benefit, in the loss" (Holland et al., 2006, p. 175). So how does this process of meaning-making work?

HOW WE THINK

How one understands each loss is part of an ongoing evolution in the way in which meaning itself is made. As a meaning-making system, the self undergoes regular and predictable changes in which former losses are resolved and the possibility of experiencing new ones is created. All of us have had the experience as adults of visiting some place that was previously only a childhood memory. Many of us, after a long absence, have even returned to visit our elementary schools only to be surprised at how small everything had become: "Omigosh, the desks have shrunk!" Visits to a childhood home, a favorite packaged food from one's childhood, even adults last encountered in childhood seem to shrink before our very eyes when first revisited in adulthood. Of course, the logic is easily reversed as we consider the absurdity of our observation. Thus it is that the desk of our childhood hasn't shrunk, rather it is we who have grown, both physically and cognitively. But how are we to explain this "phenomenon of the shrinking desk"?

It is not, as some theorists suggest, that we store accurate replicas of objects we encounter for later retrieval. Rather, memories are made of relationships between the observer and the observed. Armed with a more advanced system for making meaning of our experience, we nonetheless retrieve the artifacts of childhood with the cognitive abilities of an adult. Because people actively construct their social world, their understanding of that world is not a reproduction of the world as it is but a historical narrative on the world as experienced. So it is that our understanding of the world is a narrative tale of our history with objects, physical and social, that reveals our understanding of that experience. Without intervening experience, once objects are understood, they are preserved as first encountered. In the present case, the desks as experienced in childhood are subsequently retrieved by adults.

Jean Piaget (1954/1936; 1955/1926), a Swiss biologist who conducted research on children's development, explored the idea that as biological organisms, humans inherit two basic functions: *organization* and *adaptation*. Organization refers to the tendency for all living things to attempt to order their processes; in effect, organisms organize. Once the object has been experienced, it is brought into awareness as a part of the way we think. In this way, we make meaning of our experience. The second aspect of general functioning is the tendency of living things to make modifications in response to changing environmental conditions *in anticipation of* desired outcomes. Thus, we learn through our experience with objects. So it is that the desk, once encountered, becomes a part of the way in which we think about the school and about ourselves. But what of its apparent change in size?

Cognition involves an active relating of events whereby knowing represents our efforts to make sense. As Piaget has taught us, humans bring two basic processes to bear in their efforts to make sense in the moment of their experience of loss. On the one hand, they can *assimilate* the loss into the pool of beliefs and understandings that they bring with them to this moment as expectations. Alternatively, they can *accommodate* the forms of their expectations to the forms emerging in the experience (Joseph & Linley, 2005; Neimeyer et al., 2010).

Through assimilation, relevant environmental events are modified so that they may be incorporated into existing organizational structures. Our actions on and experience of the environment result in what Piaget called *schemes*. These regulated patterns of behavior represent forms of action that have structure, that structure experience, and that are self-structuring in the sense that they organize interests and attitudes. The desk of our childhood is just such a scheme.

Much as a meal is broken down by digestion into its component proteins, fats, carbohydrates, and minerals for use by the human body, information must be modified to fit existing mental structures. In effect, assimilation makes an experience significant by making it coherent with what we already know. Play may be thought of as the ultimate assimilative activity, whereby children convert everyday objects like cardboard boxes into forts, caves, or rocket ships. And what new mother hasn't been embarrassed by her toddler calling every man they meet "Daddy"? Schemes are the raw materials which knowledge is made of over the course of our development. Incompatible situations are either distorted to conform to prior expectations or they are ignored. The most significant implication of this explanation is that the experiences of childhood are stored by children.

The desk, by way of example, was assimilated as an object *in relation to* the child's own physical size. The problem is that when we recall childhood events as adults, we fail initially to make the necessary adjustments. The desk that was "just my size" as a child, now appears to have shrunk when I re-experience it as an adult. Yet, how can we recognize this desk as our own, if the one we've stored is so much larger?

Assimilation will necessarily involve the modification of relevant features of environmental events, especially related to any perceived loss. Such modifications include minimizing the anticipated effect of the loss, finding comfort in existing cultural beliefs, reconceptualizing the loss as a gain, or even ignoring it entirely thereby retaining the existing organizational structure. In this way, assimilation makes the loss experience significant by making it coherent with what we already know to be true. Incompatible situations are either distorted to conform to prior expectations or they are ignored. It is for this reason that some individuals appear to be coping better than others who have been actively engaged in a search for meaning following a loss (Davis et al., 2000, pp. 500–501).

> Gordon had recently lost his wife through divorce, which in turn estranged him from his now former mother-in-law with whom he had enjoyed a very amicable relationship. Within a few days, his closest colleague at work took another job in a distant city, he was forced to euthanize the family dog, and his best friend was killed in a motorcycle accident. Friends, family members, and close acquaintances all recognized the tremendous strain he was under and yet were puzzled by his general lack of obvious grief—no crying, no apparent sadness, no excessive drinking, nor even public acknowledgment of the many losses. Among the many who confronted him about his behavior, I pressed him to acknowledge the loss, "to deal with it or suffer the consequences." "Listen," he demanded of me. "Every day at the same time, I pack up my Jeep with fishing gear, load my canoe on the roof, and head out on the same road, to the same pond, put the canoe in at the same place, and paddle out to the same spot. With rod in hand and no bait on the line, I cast into the water, over and over putting each thought as it comes to me into that water until they're all gone. And for remainder of the day, I rest secure knowing where all those thoughts, all those feelings, all those memories of good times long past are safe and will be there when I visit tomorrow. You mourn in your way and leave me to mourn in mine."

Accommodation, on the other hand, will necessarily involve modifying, reorganizing, or even abandoning existing beliefs to suit the demands presented by the loss experience. Rather than altering schemas to reflect the world more accurately, however, accommodations arise from the failure of existing schemes to provide a reliable system for navigating current experience. As such, schemas are not internalized structures of the world as it is. Rather, they are cognitive representations of past experiences that shape unobservable expectations regarding future behavior. Critically, these new schemas needn't necessarily lead to more accurate representations of reality, only the expectation of more viable means for navigating an indeterminate future.

> Milly was only eleven when her "much older sister" Pam left home for marriage. Happy for her sister, she resented nonetheless being "abandoned" and "left alone" to do all the household chores. "How will I manage . . . " she asked Milly, suppressing the need to end that sentence with "without you to guide me?" "You'll be fine," Pam replied. "You're the big girl in the family now. I

know you can do it; you've always been so much help to me," came the reassurance. "Besides, you can always call whenever."

Comforted by her sister's offer of continuing support, Emily began to consider the opportunity her new role afforded. After all, Pam was leaving home
not Milly, and she felt ready, if not entirely prepared to take on the challenge of
replacing her sister. In time, household tasks became routine, her parents proved
to be far more supportive than she had imagined, and she felt a renewed sense
of self-confidence as she grew into her new role in the family.

In accommodation, modifications are made in our mental organization in
response to environmental demands. Just as the stomach and intestines tend
to change in response to demands made on the body through the ingestion
of food, so too, existing mental structures tend to be modified to suit the
demands of the environment. Although schemes are the raw materials that
knowledge is made from, later schemes grow out of earlier ones. Not mere
increases in information or content knowledge, these later schemes evidence
an increased capacity for meaning-making.

In its extreme, accommodation is essentially imitation. In this way, children learn the linguistic pattern and unique pronunciation of selected words
spoken by those around them, adopt the customs modeled by the adults in
their community, and come to share common beliefs about the nature of God,
for example. In the "mistaken" identity example above, the mother explained
to her child that the individual in question was indeed a "man," not all men
look alike, and not all who look alike are "Daddy." Armed with new information, the child was enabled to modify previously held understanding of
the concept in favor of a new and more specific understanding, much to the
delight of mom *and* dad. In the case of the desk, our adult way of thinking
corrected our childhood perceptions *in the face of* the same object.

The example of the desk, or any physical event, is a common one. Have
you ever noticed that the snowfall is never as deep as "when we were kids?"
Or that adults with whom we have had limited contact as we grow up appear
to be shorter upon meeting them than we remember? My grandfather's barn
was gigantic when we played in it as children, but it had shrunk to something
barely larger than a big garage when we returned to see it many years later.
Such experiences aren't limited to physical objects, of course. Unlike children, teenagers are less concerned with objects per se than they are with the
abstract properties of objects. To push the comparison further, adolescents
concern themselves more with the relationships between objects than with
the objects themselves. This heightened concern is especially true when these
objects are persons. Because adolescent experience is essentially interpersonal, they are interested in the form and shape of relationships, especially
between themselves and others. It is no wonder that they spend so much of

their time talking with and about others. The experiences of adolescence, therefore, are stored by adolescents. As a result, we tend to remember as adults *how* rather than *who* we were with others in high school, for example, happy, accepted, distant, or "cool."

Not all childhood experiences, once assimilated, are necessarily accommodated once encountered in later life, however. Many of the problems encountered by adults arise from the failure to reconstruct childhood schemes. In this way, childhood trauma and romantic ideals are preserved into adulthood without the challenge that can come from contradictory experience. Many a first marriage is tested in this way by the collision of competing ideals concerning the form and structure of the "perfect relationship" borne of one's experience of families in childhood.

Sharon came to see me for the express purpose of examining her changing relationship with her husband following the recent birth of their first child. She explained that she was the second of seven children and had a life-long pattern of taking on tasks for others. Having married "to get out of the house from under the burden of caring for the children," she reports assuming major responsibility in her marriage and in life generally. Weary from the routine, she has become tired of "being in charge" and "fed up, resentful, and angry." In due course, we developed the analogy that her life was much like carrying a pile of neatly arranged bricks, not all of which she had stacked, but all of which she felt compelled to carry. She complained of having to do for everyone, of having to constantly "pick up after" her husband, of not having enough time for herself, and of increasing apathy related to her work. She found herself crying "for no apparent reason" and frustrated to levels that were atypical for her. Angry for having, as she viewed it, to "raise two children" (i.e., her child and her husband), she was having difficulty relating to some co-workers, especially those who are demanding or "so damned helpless."

Over the course of our work together, she explored the losses associated with the loss of her dream family and its general connection with the larger picture of her life—work, family of origin, and identity. Comfortable with the realization that her husband was neither going to change nor reconcile, she sought a divorce. She began to consider her future behavior related to becoming more spontaneous and her "dread fear of losing control" as revealed in dreams about tornadoes and hurricanes. She recognized her great need to be in control also limited her capacity to be helped by others, making her appear invulnerable and cold. At the conclusion of our sessions over a year, she had developed a clear idea of the future direction for her career and had formulated detailed plans for achieving her vocational goals. She expressed confidence in raising her child and was gaining a greater understanding of her developing relationship with her former spouse. She felt confident in her decision to accept her parents "for who they are" and to seek fulfillment in other more reciprocal relationships.

As Sharon's struggle illustrates, the narratives we carry with us from child-hood exercise a profound effect on how we understand and behave in similar contexts in adulthood. Without intervening and contradictory experience with alternative familial and interpersonal relationships, our assumptions about "how things are supposed to be" can go unchallenged. As further illustrated, however, dysfunctional childhood schemes once recognized can be modified when confronted by alternative experiences in adulthood. The possible resurgence of grief and the opportunity to reconstruct prior meanings accompanies each developmental advance in the individual's system for making sense of the event. This resurgence can mean living and reliving the events of a prior loss as new circumstances bring us face to face with the reality of losses yet unexperienced. As Neubert (2009) reflects, "life remains perilous, no matter how elaborated and sophisticated our symbolic systems of prediction and control may be" (p. 175).

FINDING A BALANCE

Because assimilation and accommodation are complementary processes that occur simultaneously, they must necessarily be in balance if adaptation is to occur. In organizing our experience, we must simultaneously assimilate novel experiences into pre-existing structures and accommodate pre-existing struc-tures to meet the demands presented by new environmental conditions. In this way, prior meanings are continuous with the meanings we make of our current experience and influence our expectations for the future. In effect, changing circumstances encourage us to make modifications to ensure a desired future. Disequilibration serves as a stimulus to development, while equilibration is its goal. As such, humans operate as self-organizing systems. Each person's self-regulating system emerges as a consequence of new states of equilibrium that were created by the previous self-regulatory system. In this way, we are modified by every experience whether we notice the change or not.

Development can be seen from this view as the natural outcome of our attempts to make stable sense of a changing world. In effect, we must change in order to remain the same. As a result of this recurring cycle of equilibra-tion-disequilibration-equilibration, development takes a path that may best be described by a spiral. The outer turns are analogous to the person's attempts at the integration of novel experiences into existing structures. In each turn, the spiral moves to a new level of organization analogous to the movement to a higher stage of development.

THE RECONSTRUCTIVE SELF

"Who are you?" said the Caterpillar. . . . "I—I hardly know, Sir, just at present," Alice replied rather shyly, "at least I know who I was when I got up this morning, but I think I must have changed several times since then." (Carroll, 1960, p. 47)

In many ways, life is like a do-it-yourself kit that comes with most of the parts and few of the directions. Faced with the challenge to live our lives in a sea of change, we are called upon to build ourselves from the raw materials of our experience with life itself. People are active agents in their own development. Seen in this way, development is neither wholly a consequence of events that have happened to us nor wholly the result of inner urgings. Instead, human development is the consequence of a complex interaction of factors, not the least of which are our own attempts to organize the experience.

Inherent in human nature are certain structuring tendencies. We attempt to make sense of changes within ourselves and in our experience of the world in which we live. Think back to how often since you began reading this chapter that you have stopped to consider the meaning of what you've been reading. Even now, you may be asking yourself: "What does this mean?" The point is that as humans, we are always trying to make sense. As Kegan (1982) explains:

> What a human organism organizes is meaning. Thus, it is not that a person makes meaning, as much as that the activity of being person is the activity of meaning-making. And the most fundamental thing we do with what happens to us is organize it. We literally make sense. (p. 11)

As change brings loss to our lives, we are faced with the challenge to make sense of that loss. And in our attempts to do so, we are challenged to rethink who we are. In this way, human development represents the course of our attempts to make sense of those changes going on around us.

THE COURSE OF DEVELOPMENT

Understanding human development helps to situate people within the larger social context within which development takes place. For the purposes of this book, development is conceptualized as a qualitative property of people themselves, where change is directed to balancing the tension created by forces for differentiation and integration. Understanding the regularity with which thinking changes provides a valuable framework for the study of reactions to loss.

Based on their extensive review of the literature on children's notions of death, Maria Krepia and her colleagues (Krepia et al., 2017) concluded that the child's understanding develops slowly, is formed by multiple factors, and is structured by various partial notions. They identified a host of factors that contribute to forming a mature concept of death. Among the most determining of these factors are age, cognitive development, prior experiences of death, and the social environment of family, school, and religion. Although age serves as a practical guide in predicting a child's level of understanding through the elementary grades, beyond ages 8 or 9, children's development becomes more and more variable (Kenyon, 2001).

Changes in children's understandings of death and related losses can more reliably be explained by the developmental level of how they think about, reason, and problem-solve. Each level provides a particular frame of reference for meaning-making. Each succeeding level represents the capacity to make sense of a greater variety of experiences in a more adequate way. In this way, development represents successively more complex attempts to make meaning of the facts of one's social experience. Nonetheless, because the sets of events from which one composes a life are experienced uniquely, each person's life can be viewed as its own grand narrative.

Because the cognitive functioning of a child at a given age is subject to the wide array of contributing factors noted above, it's more accurate to see cognitive development as a process of increased capacity to draw upon a variety of strategies for solving problems. Movement to higher levels of cognitive development can be understood as expanding our repertoire of possible approaches to problem solving. As we age, our experience with loss expands and with it come advances in the range and variability of coping strategies available for problem solving. These advances can be conceptualized as regular patterns of change, especially notable in children's thinking about loss and related events.

Recall that Piaget was interested in how children understand themselves and the world around them. His genius lay in his ability to recognize the underlying logic in children's efforts to solve everyday problems. In understanding children's moral development, for example, he watched them play marbles and asked them "Where do the rules come from?" "Can they ever be changed?" or "What makes the rules fair?" (Piaget, 1965/1932). Based on his experiences with children, Piaget identified four major periods of development, which represent general changes in the child's way of knowing.

Piaget used the term *stage* to refer to qualitative differences in the way people think, where each stage represents an individual frame of reference for meaning-making. Each succeeding stage represents the capacity to make sense of a greater variety of experience in a more adequate way. The fundamental reason for movement from one stage to the next is that a later stage is more adequate in problem-solving than an earlier stage.

The first of these stages, the *sensorimotor* period, occupies approximately the first two years of life. The child's interactions with the environment are characterized by *actions on objects* and involve sensory and motor movements. A significant outcome of this period is the development of the concept of *object permanence* which allows the child to recognize that objects continue to exist outside of the child's presence and thus can be lost.

The second stage, the *pre-operational* period, which extends from approximately age two through seven, is marked by the development of language and the *symbolic function*. The child's interactions involve *actions on symbols*, which permit the representational interactions that allow words to be used to create language. The outcomes of this period include the notion of cause-effect relationships, a movement between different viewpoints, and the notion that an object has its own identity despite changes in its appearance. What has been lost, can now be found.

The *concrete operational* period extends from approximately age seven through age twelve. Its distinguishing feature, and hence its name, is the development of operational thought. An *operation* is an internalized action that is part of an organized structure. Interactions during this period involve *operations upon objects* which permit the child to classify objects and to seriate objects or events in their proper order. Perhaps the most important development of this period is *conservation*, the ability to maintain relationships between objects despite their physical manipulation. The ability to conserve permits the child to perceive a certain stability about the world and to make plans for the future. In this way, things that change are not necessarily lost but only different. Children in this period begin to take the thoughts and intentions of others into account when interacting with others. Although concrete operational thinkers can appreciate lawful nature in the events of the world, their thinking is limited by the concrete reality of what *is* rather than by the abstract reality of what *could be.*

The last of Piaget's stages, the *formal operational* period, does not typically begin before age twelve. In this period individuals begin to exhibit the kind of abstract thinking that is characterized by a hypothesis-testing approach to problem solving. Thinking involves *operations on symbols* which allows the individual to consider things as they are as only one of many alternative potential solutions to a problem. Loss can now be understood as the death of possibility, including the loss of an imagined future.

T. J. was forced to relocate closer to his parents following the death of his wife and the consequent reduction in household income and the need to find reliable childcare for his three children. Beyond the lingering sense of abandonment and loss felt by each of the children regarding their mother, each of the children was struggling in their own way with the impending reality of moving to a new home. Bonnie (age 5) wanted to know if she had been a "bad girl" and declared that she just wasn't going to move; Waylon (age 9) wondered if this meant he would have to give up his role in the upcoming school play, or cancel his impending birthday celebration, or find a whole new set of friends to replace the old ones; and, Jimmie (age 13) was concerned that his friends would think that he had abandoned them or worse, would pity him and his dad as "some los- ers" who couldn't take the loss. How was T. J. to address the concerns of each of these children in a way each would understand? How would he help Bonnie to understand that she hadn't caused her mother's death or the family to move, or help Waylon to regain control over the changes the move would bring, or help Jimmie to appreciate that how his friends might react wasn't necessarily inevitable or even true?

Clearly, caregivers should be at least at the same level as their charges if they are to understand fully the nature of the child's concerns as the child understands them. I will have more to say about matching interventions to the developmental levels of children and adolescents in subsequent chapters. For now, it is important to emphasize that caregivers should be capable of more complex levels of thought if they are to be most effective in helping children and adolescents to consider alternative solutions to their current life questions.

SELF AND SOCIETY

It is important to note that while the construction of reality may be a subjec- tive accomplishment, it is not a random one. Because individuals tend both to adapt and to organize, they must necessarily interact with their environments. Instead, development takes place in a social context. The process of knowing emerges in the light of interactions between ourselves and our surroundings. Thus, person and world are not separate, nor even in interaction, but rather are inextricably linked in *transactions* with one another (Kraus, 2015; Mead, 1934; Raskin, 2015; Riegel, 1979; Vygotsky, 1978). We construct reality from our personal experience and that reality represents a relationship between our self and the world as we experience that world. Our personal relationships with others emerge from a lifetime of successive, qualitative differentiations of our selves from the world. In so doing, we must necessarily give up who we are (i.e., the self that has served us to this point) and acknowledge that who-I-have-been is no longer who-I-am-about-to-become.

Heather was struggling with her relationship with other members of her group of graduate students—trying to sort out who she was, who she had been and no longer wanted to be, and who she wanted to be but couldn't yet find the way to become—when she wrote in her journal: "I want to move beyond this space, to a space where others' feelings won't bring out such negative feelings in me. But I want to do this without shutting people down. Maybe the way to do this is to feel what I feel, to share my feelings without the judging aspect of others, and just to let it go to make room for another new experience to move along my path. I don't feel comfortable in my ability to be this way; it seems that no matter how hard I try I still want people to hear my hurt and make amends somehow. I find this way of being very elusive. I seem to feel that I know the way, but it is as if my path is through a dark forest, and I keep searching for a sun-drenched pasture to appear. As if there is truly a clearly defined, unambiguous way to navigate through life and all the relationships that make-up my life. I want deep relationships without conflict, as if conflict were a negative way of being instead of an opportunity for intimacy. Maybe the way to increased intimacy is to be in conflict, to provide the opportunity for me to shed more light on my path. How will I let go of my 'past' that has led me deeper into the forest unless I let myself 'be' in a way that doesn't feel comfortable and normal? What a perverse feeling of comfort and normality this idea brings!

"Writing out my thoughts seems to clear the air, to make sense of my experience, to allow me to see all the gray areas in my thoughts. To see that my old view of the world as 'black or white' is false. I have actually 'known' this fact cognitively for a long time, but the experience with my group is showing me that I can live in the gray, that the world won't end if each situation cannot only be seen as black or white. Trying to control it all takes too much energy and stifles creativity and hence the experience. Where am I headed? Where will I end up? What difference does it make? At this moment of clarity at least, I feel that all that is important is the trip."

Development involves the loss of the old self and with it a way of knowing the world that no longer works. In its place a new balance emerges. Thus, development involves a sort of coming through the problem to a new integration that gives us a new direction for future growth. As Heather's example demonstrates, cognition is more than what a person knows. Cognitions represent internally organized systems of relations, which comprise a set of rules for processing information or connecting events in personal experience. From this view, cognitive thinking is the active relating of events.

People are social beings who use their experiences with one another to confirm the utility of their constructions. Facts represent socially constructed representations of linguistic artifacts where language is the primary means by which to share that reality with others. Accepting that we can never really know the truth of what happens, truth lies in the intersubjectivity of the collected truths we bring to understanding the world of our own varied experiences. In effect, when it comes to reality, we "cut a deal" with one another to talk about the world by naming things and then acting as if they are real. Accepting that reality is our personal construction does not eliminate the possibility of some objective reality. What it does is make such a notion irrelevant, much like asking an atheist if God is a woman. Our facts are derived from the theories we've built up about the world. Thus, the best we can hope for in understanding one another is a reliable, rather than a verifiable, road map to guide our future interactions.

And when the reality our constructions map onto our experience fails us, we can change that map in an attempt to better navigate future interactions. In this way, our constructions map our current experience while offering hypotheses on the course ahead only to be tested by subsequent experience. We act as if things are true, until they "prove" to us they are not. Creating new meaning structures in discourse with others permits experience to be considered from multiple perspectives. New meanings offer the possibility of resolving problems previously thought unmanageable. From this perspective, engaging people in collaboration to determine the most workable course of action under today's conditions offers the hope of a more complex but relatively stable system for negotiating the boundaries of one's experience tomorrow.

When we talk to another person, we actually ask the other to be different than he or she was before we began. We also take the risk to change ourselves as well. That is the tension created in any social situation. Communication invites change. Person and world are inextricably linked in transactions with one another by which we come to know our environment—a two-way movement of phenomena between ourselves and this reality we can never know directly. In Dewey's (1933/1910) language, we *do* things to the world and then we *undergo* the consequences.

As social beings, therefore, we are faced with the enduring problems associated with building effective relationships. As noted earlier, in choosing to behave in one way toward another, I not only reveal the kind of person I am, but also the kind of person I want to be. And concurrently, how one reacts to my behavior reveals themselves and shapes how we are to be in a relationship with one another. As meaning-makers, we are embedded in a continuous process of negotiation and renegotiation of who we are and who we are in relation to others. And at each juncture in these negotiations, we are faced with calculating the cost of losing one's self in taking the leap to become a new self yet unknown. Complicating this calculation is the reality that there are things that we "know" of which we are unaware—assumptive realities formed long ago that have withstood disconfirmation and which have become so "normalized" as to be persistently out of awareness.

Accepting the notion that all knowledge is the outcome of our efforts to make meaning of our unique experience means that for any event there may potentially be multiple realities and that each individual's knowledge is idiosyncratic. What we are left with is the challenge to make sense of these multiple "realities." Recognizing that we experience the world in different ways on different occasions acknowledges that we are defined by a multiplicity of social relationships that depend, in part, upon where we stand at the time. The point is that our identities, who we are and how we are in relation to others, are subject to change. And as we have seen in Chapter 1, the loss that accompanies these changes subjects us to the possibility that our identities, the selves we have chosen and to which we are committed, will be thrown out of balance. As we have also seen, not all those choices were entirely of our own making. Personal circumstances, social institutions, and chance encounters have all played their parts in the construction of the social narratives we claim as our own life stories. Just as our choices reveal the kind of self we have been, so they reveal a potential future self.

In the course of our evolution toward a new, more socially-aware self, each choice that expands the range of our experience with those unlike ourselves offers the opportunity to expand our assumptive cultural boundaries and challenges us to give up a familiar past. Confronting one's own prejudices can be a journey of discovery as part of an ongoing evolution in the way in which meaning itself is made. By attending to the surprise that is occasioned by our encounters with Others, we can challenge the illusion of our omnipotence. In so doing, we take the risk to build a more competent self that can make better sense of the world of which we are all a part.

IN PASSING

The central argument of this book is that humans are meaning makers who are continuously engaged in attempts to make sense of their experiences within themselves in an ever-changing world. The resulting basic mental structures are continually being reorganized and redefined through exercise and confrontation by opposing ideas. These meanings comprise the cognitive categories that make up a person's view of reality, that give direction to future action, and that structure the interpretation and application of knowledge. In this view, development is seen as the natural outcome of our attempts to make stable sense of a changing world. In our efforts to maintain a balance between the world as we have known it and our current experience of that world, we must change in order to remain the same. In effect, changing circumstances encourage us to make modifications to ensure a desired future. Thus, humans adapt to enhance their potential to reap positive outcomes from an anticipated environment.

The inevitability of change brings loss to the mind of the person who can appreciate that things are somehow different. Determining what is different is central to and initiates the meaning-making process. Critically, this process of negotiating challenge, change, and loss does not end with adolescence, nor does the development of our understanding of the world and the meaning we give to our experience of it. As we have seen in Sharon's case, interpretation of the loss event will change as individual circumstances and the level of meaning-making shift over time. Moreover, developmental research supports the possibility of further development in adulthood and continued advances in the ability to make meaning of oneself and to reinterpret prior experiences in new ways (Kegan & Lahey, 2016; Manners et al., 2004; Torbert, 1994). Continued development notwithstanding, whatever logic one brings to making meaning, each loss challenges the illusion of our omnipotence and threatens to destroy our very being. In learning to mourn the outgrown self that each loss leaves behind, we can each develop the courage to become the person that lies ahead.

Understanding that reality is constructed by the individual opens the way to autonomy as the recognition of one's ownership of his or her particular reality. Understanding that problems represent unsuccessful attempts to resolve difficulties helps point to potential limitations in one's current way of knowing—of the essential process of making meaning itself. The problem is that the self as a construction cannot see itself. All is not lost, however. As von Glasersfeld (1984) explained, "the operations by means of which we assemble our experiential world can be explored, and that an awareness of this operating . . . can help us to do it differently and, perhaps, better" (p. 18). In exploring how we create our experiential world, we can increase our awareness of both the limitations and opportunities that our present understanding provides. Recognizing that we cannot escape our own constructed reality, we may come closer to living the truth we attempt to understand.

In chapter 1, we saw how important loss is as a necessary consequence of living so as to care about others. In the present chapter, it has been shown how our understanding of loss is transformed over time and how loss can be a stimulant to further development. If we recall that caring involves the interpenetration of the self with other selves, we can understand the significance of care for stimulating development in the context of loss. In the pages to follow, we will look at how caregivers can become developmental educators by applying this understanding to help others learn from their losses. We will also take a closer look at how children and adolescents come to understand their world and the associated losses that predictably shape their understanding of themselves in that world. Finally, we will examine how such understanding can help adults understand the influence of past losses in their own lives and how that understanding can help them build a more reliable self for negotiating the world ahead.

NOTE

Adapted from R. L. Hayes. (1984). Coping with loss: A developmental approach to helping children and youth. *Counseling and Human Development, 17*(3), 1–12. Love Publishing, the rightsholder on record for this title, has ceased operation. Current rightsholder is unknown despite best efforts to identify; R. L. Hayes. (2020). *Making meaning: A constructivist approach to counseling and groupwork in education.* Washington, DC: Lexington/Rowman & Littlefield. Republished with permission of Lexington/Rowman & Littlefield.

Chapter 3

Mediating in Loss

Clients who come to counseling often find themselves in the throes of an identity crisis, wondering "Who am I?" "Where am I going in life?" "What will I become?" Clients enter counseling with meaning systems that have failed to support their efforts to make sense. In understanding their efforts at making meaning, the focus should be more on present understanding in the service of future actions than on past actions in the service of present understanding. Questioning intended to uncover meaning construction helps in responding to very real concerns and failed expectations. Such is the hope of any client who comes to counseling: to be understood and to find new meaning to direct future action. It is assumed that people do the best that they can at any moment given their situation and the constraints of their constructs. Because the past is reconstructed in the present, the resources people need lie within their own personal histories. Thus, in caring for others, strengths and resources should be emphasized and presenting problems accepted as "real" for the person. Of course, the real world matters, but it is our interpretation of our experience in that world that gives meaning to our actions.

If we understand a problem as the difference between the *world-as-we-know-it* and the *world-as-we-would-like-it-to-be*, then problems reveal discrepancies between challenges and capacities. Basically, problems represent unsuccessful attempts to resolve difficulties in understanding. Seen in this way, problems provide clues to the logic of the individual's meaning-making system and point to limitations in current ways of knowing. Recognizing that we cannot escape our own constructed reality, counseling is intended to create the conditions for exploring how clients create their experiential world. In building the proper context for change, caregivers should provide opportunities for clients to be at their best in a supportive social setting. Rather than conceal clients' genius and reveal their disabilities, counseling should reveal their genius and minimize their disabilities.

Because humans are self-organizing systems, they have considerable powers of spontaneous recuperation. As such, people make the best choices available to them at any given time. From this perspective, people are accepted as operating out of their own internal maps. How one makes meaning of experience betrays the underlying logic of how one makes sense of one's own existence. It is to the client's struggle to understand the self and others, in the context of a shared social experience, that caregivers should turn their attention.

RECONCEPTUALIZING COUNSELING

In caring for others, the approach shifts from studying *what* the person knows to *how* the person is *knowing* it. As presented in chapter 1, it is the difference between studying "made" meanings and studying meaning-making. Rather than ignore the client's social environment, "it is not sufficient to only observe under *which* circumstances a person is living, but it is of special interest to examine *how* this person *experiences* these circumstances" (Kraus, 2015, part 5, para. 3).

The inevitability of change challenges our understanding of that world and gives rise to what we experience as loss. People resist change because it would mean inviting the possibility that some (all!) of their presumptive assumptions about the world are not only false but will need to be replaced by a new reality. The possibility of changing how one thinks can threaten to destroy the system of relationships that bind those things already "known" to be true. As presented in chapter 1, the threat is the possibility of losing the self or foregoing the possibility for greater autonomy. The resulting ambivalence and hostility are less about resistance to becoming empowered as they are about sustaining the integrity of the self-system. Such is the nature of loss, the challenge to see the world differently, and the realization that the world will be different only if we change. Confronting oneself and others makes oneself vulnerable to change and means taking the risk to build a more stable relationship at the cost of losing the present one.

Angel and Andre were referred to me by their employment counselor to address their supervisor's repeated complaints regarding their "disruptive behavior at work." According to the referral, they were recently married, and both were employed in the same division at a local automotive plant. Although assigned to different offices, they had frequent contact with one another that often resulted in "loud and angry disputes." Following the customary intake questions and a review of my role in our work together, I asked "What brings the two of you here today?" "Whoa," Angel responded quickly, "there's no 'two' of us here. We're here because he doesn't do his job." And without hesitation, Andre responded, "And there you go again with that 'it's all on you crap.'"

After listening to them spar for a few minutes about who was responsible for what and how things might be better if only the other would "do things right," I interrupted. "Am I correct that you were sent to me to address some complaints about your behavior at work?" After nods from both, I asked, "And is what has been going on between the two of you for the past few minutes typical of what has led to these complaints?" Of course, there was much to disentangle here, but in their brief exchange I was able to see firsthand what they came to understand about themselves. Each was a perfectionist who carried that value proudly into the workplace. And each, in their perfection, was certain that how they do things is right and correct. And each, during their encounters with one another in the workplace, had occasion to be critical of the other's behavior. And fearing the disapproval of co-workers given their marriage to one another, each was certain to let everyone know "that's not how I would do it." Over several sessions, we explored: what sense each made of being referred to mediation; how each decided what was "right"; how each decided what course of action to take in retaliation; what impact they imagined their behavior had on others, especially each other; what it would mean for each of them to change; and what possible futures they imagined for dealing with one another in the workplace and at home.

In time, they each came to understand the source of their need to "get things right" and how each saw the other's "wrong" behavior as a reflection on themselves. Unwilling to accept any compromise and the loss of self-esteem that would bring, they decided to divorce, accepting that the confrontational character they had initially admired in each other was both projection and untenable in their marriage. And certain in their assumptions, they determined to just avoid each other at work.

Despite my hope for a change in behavior to accommodate new understandings of themselves and their impact on others, neither Angel nor Andre viewed their conflicts and problems as opportunities for growth. New understandings were assimilated into existing structures, and new behaviors were designed to protect rather than challenge current understanding. Each viewed their behavior as "somebody else's problem" and resolved to avoid situations that would give rise to what each saw as "a losing battle." Their efforts to reestablish equilibrium lessened the urgency to change. In effect, Angel and Andre stopped being with each other so that each would not have to change and risk the loss of an identity so carefully constructed.

Although clients typically come to counseling in search of answers to their questions, caregivers are encouraged to shift their attention from changing what clients believe to varying the process by which clients arrive at those beliefs. From this perspective, caregivers should be less concerned with what their clients believe to be true, or with why they believe it, and more with how they came to believe it. Taking this approach involves trying to understand how the client makes sense of personal experience. Questions directed at

uncovering clients' understanding of their own personal history will necessarily ask: "How did you decide to take this or that course of action? How do
you know this is true?" The client's "resistance" to any interpretation by the
caregiver reflects natural self-protective processes that guard the integrity of
the individual's meaning-making system. Accordingly, resistance needs to be
worked *with* not overcome as the caregiver attempts to understand the client's
experience rather than trying to change or control it. Caregiving should provide a safe harbor for a person's efforts to make meaning in the face of crisis,
which *is* the transformation of meaning and a movement toward growth. In
working with others as part of the change process, Heifetz and Linsky (2004)
caution caregivers not to underestimate the familiar:

> [instead], you need to respect and acknowledge the loss that people suffer when
> you ask them to leave behind something they have lived with for years. It is not
> enough to point to a hopeful future. People need to know that you realize that
> the change you are asking them to make is difficult and that what you are asking
> them to give up has real value to them. (p. 36)

THE DEATH OF EXPERTISE

In caring for others, avoid the self-deception that it is your knowledge and
expertise that leads to successful therapeutic outcomes. Instead, consider
multiple potential interpretations of any behavior and collaborate with
clients in the construction of new and more viable alternative meanings.
Understanding how people come to know helps in appreciating another's
reality. Understanding leads to better predictions about the direction to take
in improving our relationship with them and their relationships with others.
From this perspective, prevention gives way to development as an organizing
principle for counseling. If, as caregivers, we are to assist others in transcending the losses they encounter in the course of living, then our efforts should
focus on development and the person's experience of this process.

The reality that professional caregivers (e.g., counselors, psychologists,
social workers, psychiatrists, clergy) generally interact with their clients indi-
vidually and/or in small groups leaves them to make sense of their clients'
idiosyncratic behaviors in the context of generalized human functioning.
Critically, theorists (Gibson & McDaniel, 2010; Heine, 2011; Overton &
Muller, 2013; Siegler et al., 2017; Syed et al., 2018) today are less sanguine
about the possibility of discovering psychological universals. Instead, they
are focused more on the influence of cultural variables in the explanation
of developmental phenomena. Indeed, cross-culture evidence suggests that

"theories do not have to be objectively true to facilitate healing" (Hansen, 2006, p. 293). As Maturana and Varela (1992) argue,

[the knowledge of knowledge] compels us to adopt an attitude of permanent vigilance against the temptation of certainty. It compels us to recognize that certainty is not proof of truth. It compels us to realize that the world everyone sees is not *the* world but *a* [emphases in original] world which we bring forth with others. (p. 245)

Rather than accepting a particular theory as an explanation, think of it instead as a viewpoint, a lens that offers a particular perspective on understanding one's experience. For our purposes, that lens is focused on one's efforts to make meaning of experience, especially with others, in a world of our own making. Rather than operating from a particular theory, I accept the position that theories are not fixed realities but rather are narrative structures that offer a variety of potential explanations for the creation of new meanings. As caregivers, we can access the life as experienced by the client only indirectly as communicated by the client. Moreover, and despite our professional preparation, we do not access our clients' experience objectively, but filter it through our own understanding leaving both parties with little more than a reciprocal interpretation of events. Rather than intervene as *experts* in the lives of individuals we might regard as autonomous human beings, we should approach our clients as *collaborators* who are embedded in a social context with other *human beings*. From this perspective, counseling and psychotherapy may properly be understood as a process of consultation whereby the caregiver and client system collaborate in the co-construction of potential solutions to client-defined problems. In this spirit of collaboration, Attig (2011) offers some guidance for the caregiver:

Caregivers should resist any temptation to attempt to do the difficult work of coping for us when we are bereaved. Our coping with loss is a personal experience, as is all coping. No other person can grieve for us. The challenge is ours to meet, the choices are ours to make. . . . Although the grieving is ours and ours alone to do, we need not grieve alone, and those who care about us can help us in all of these ways as we relearn our worlds. (p. 23)

MEDIATING IN LOSS

The loss brought on by change creates a gap between the self that is *no longer me* and the new self that is *not yet me*. Once the feelings associated with loss have been acknowledged, intervention should seek to *mediate* between the loss and the person's experience. It is in this *zone of proximal development*

(Vygotsky, 1978) that clients can be helped to make better meaning of their experience. In caregiving, this process becomes a kind of *mediated learning experience* in which the interactions of the caregiver and the client increase the capacity of the individual to change in the direction of greater adaptability. Recognizing that the client's understanding of the past is socially constructed in the present, especially in the presence of the caregiver, the caregiver should be more concerned with *how* rather than *what* or *why* clients believe as they do.

Acknowledging that reality as one knows it is socially constructed is to recognize the dual nature of the self as defined in relationship to the other. In other words, objects are defined (in part) by their relationship to each other. Understood in this way, all relationships can be seen as being defined by a kind of reciprocal causality by which each behavior needs the logical complement of the other. Thus, one can continue in the role of caregiver only if it is complemented by the role of the client, and vice versa. More generally, caregiving demands someone to care for. In that process, caring exacts particular behaviors on the part of caregivers if they are to be responsive to the unique concerns of the other.

THE LANGUAGE OF CARE

Critical to our understanding of the counseling relationship is the position that observer and the object of observation (i.e., counselor vs. client) are interrelated. In this relationship, the findings of the investigation (i.e., diagnosis) are created in the process of the observation (i.e., counseling) (Krauss, 2005). "There is a kind of co-authoring happening between client and counselor that implies both that the client is active, and that the counselor assists with an alternative storyline if an injurious, non-resilient narrative is told" (Wheat & Whiting, 2018, p. 103).

As presented, humans are biological organisms engaged in making meaning of their experience in efforts to realize a more stable and reliable understanding of the world. Critically, this development of greater understandings takes place within a social context that is itself changed by our interactions with others. To find one's place in such a world requires the development of a reliable, consensual system for grounding understanding of the self in relation to others. Language enables such negotiation by providing a symbol system for expressing sets of assumptions about one's understanding of that world. Because people actively construct their social world, their personal narratives are not so much a record of their life experience as they are a living representation of how they are experiencing life.

Language does not permit the accurate representation of a world "out there," but rather is a symbol system for expressing sets of assumptions about our understanding of that world. As argued in the previous chapter, we "cut a deal" with one another to talk about the world by naming things and then acting as if they are real. Note, for example, how those who accept an objective reality support a language wherein one has "viewpoints" rather than "opinions," or "takes a perspective" rather than "has a bias," or refers to clients as being "seen" rather than "related to," or where saying "I see" means "I understand." Rather than take the position that "seeing is believing," one might say instead that "believing is seeing." It is in this way that language shapes our conversations. Language does not mimic reality; rather, language constitutes reality, with each language constructing specific aspects of reality, each in its own way. Whether one speaks of a loss as such directly or instead through oblique references to a "passing," "defeat," "waste," "wreck," or "hurt," as examples, tells us much about how clients understand their loss. In attempting to understand the client's actions, therefore, caregivers should ask themselves "Given all the things this person might have said or done, who would say or do such a thing?"

SURPRISE AND SELF-REFLECTION

If we accept the possibility of multiple realities, we must necessarily be self-reflective. Faced with the recurring possibility of error, caregivers (no less than their clients) should engage in the process of continual self-reflection (Ferreira et al., 2017; Gilbert & Sliep, 2009; Jensen, 2007; Knapp et al., 2017; Schon 1987). The recognition of one's own failed expectations—that sense of surprise—indicates the necessity to re-examine one's own beliefs and to reconsider one's values.

When supervising counseling interns, I often ask them to consider what they can tell me about, for example, a thirty-year-old client who comes to them for counseling. Predictably they respond that they would suspend judgment until they know more. "Okay," I allow, "what can you tell me if you also know the client identified as female?" And in that moment, a few will acknowledge their surprise: "Oh, I was thinking he was a man." I continue, "What if I also tell you that the client is Asian?" "Oops!" some reply. "I was thinking the client is African-American—most of our clients at the clinic are." "And if I tell you that the client is a trans woman, whose father is African-American and whose mother is Japanese," I continue, "what then?" As the students soon realize, they already believe a lot about their clients, having never met them, and are likely to act on those assumptions as they struggle with surprise after surprise. Attending to their own surprise helps them recalculate the assumptions they hold of their clients and offers the possibility of re-evaluating their expectations for the course of treatment and their role in it.

Surprise is about failed expectations. It is about how our understanding of the world that informs our experience in the moment fails us. And, in that moment, it reveals how we understand that world and what we had expected. Surprise is also about loss, however momentary, of understanding. Accepting that people are never not themselves, we can see that what surprises them and how they choose to behave reflects their understanding of others as well as themselves. By noting someone's surprise or attending to apparent disappointments, you can open the door to discovering the core of the person's meaning-making.

One needn't necessarily be trained professionally to realize the power of surprise as a gateway to revealing one's assumptions. Ask yourself: How often do you encounter people unlike yourself in the course of your daily life? What is your experience of those encounters? What sense do you make of that experience? and, What do you do with that understanding as you move forward in the rest of your day? In particular, pay attention to what surprises you in these encounters. These are often the smallest of surprises—rifts in the otherwise seamless tapestry of our assumptions about other people. Surprise is our window into the world of our own construction, that place where meaning is made and from which our expectations flow.

So it is that when a colleague is consistently late to meetings, you come to accept (like it or not) that is "just how she is." By contrast, note your surprise on the day you arrive on time and there she sits. Become aware of how often you surprise yourself in this way and consider what you had expected. As well, consider what you had assumed in explaining her behavior. Without confirming evidence, was she late because she doesn't care about the group, imagines she has more important things to do, sees her participation as irrelevant, or has competing responsibilities that interfere with being "on time?" And, of course, what's changed to bring her here today? In such moments of self-reflection, you may discover the assumptions that lie beneath and be provided an opportunity to reconstruct that experience by talking to her.

Humans are meaning-making creatures who rehearse encounters in anticipation, interpret the meaning of encounters in the moment, and reflect on the implications in retrospect. Thus, conduct and character derive from a conscious self, which becomes increasingly more stable through present reflection upon its own past conduct in the light of predicted future conditions within a social context. I know that was quite a mouthful but read it again: (1) conduct and character derive from a conscious self; (2) that self becomes increasingly more stable through reflecting on past conduct; (3) this self-reflection takes place in the context of our expectations for the future;

and (4) all this activity happens within our relationships with others. Because the client's reality represents a relationship between the client and the world as the client understands that world, true understanding combines knowledge with felt experience. What is of value is that which is thought of as making a difference in the "self." In making judgments about the people and events in one's life, therefore, one is making judgments about the kind of self one is and ought to become. By promoting self-reflection on the part of our clients about their own past behavior, we can help shape the person they will become. Once having considered how the client has behaved in particular ways in the past, attention shifts to considering who the client would like to be in the future.

CREATING A CONTEXT FOR
INDIVIDUAL RECONSTRUCTION

Accepting that reality is a self-constructive activity, caregivers should try to understand how clients make sense of personal experience—how they make meaning. Importantly, clients make meaning within a social context that is informed by their current understanding of the past and their vision for the future. Therefore, caregiving can provide the proper context for both the reconstruction of one's past understanding and the rehearsal of alternative futures.

The implication of this perspective is that caregiving should create a social context for reconstruction. This "holding environment" is what Winnicott (2002) saw as a prerequisite for healthy development by "the continuation of reliable holding in terms of the ever-widening circle of family and school and social life" (p. 238). In this context, professional caregiving is an attempt to provide an environment that acknowledges and then challenges the client's reality. As such, it supports the client's efforts to restore some balance to the world as the client knows it. In taking the perspective of the caregiver as audience to the client, clients experience themselves in new and potentially more effective ways.

Through their efforts to maintain their integrity, clients show us who they are and, by implication, how they think they can change. The sensitive caregiver will use such opportunities to acknowledge the client's reality and seek to understand its significance in the client's life. Because we do not know what we do not know, it is only through some interaction that disrupts our current understanding and our reflection upon its meaning that we come to be aware of and to understand what until now we did not.

Although we may be autonomous in our actions, our behavior is acted out in a social environment with other persons. Because people socially construct their worlds, they are always cooperating with others. Rather than intervene in the lives of individual members as autonomous human beings, therefore, caregivers should attend to their relationships with clients as co-inhabitants in a developmental context. From such a perspective, the caregiver no longer asks: "How should I relate to my clients?" or "What should be the appropriate (i.e., right) course of action (read as intervention)?" Rather, caregivers should recognize that they are already in relationships with their clients as other people. Consequently, caregivers should ask of themselves: "Who am I in this relationship? How am I relating to the other? What can I do right now to effect a change that will encourage greater understanding among (rather than between) us?" Accepting that the caregiver is part of the client's social environment, counseling from this perspective looks more like a dialogue than an interview. Consistent with Bakhtin's (1981) original formulation of the term, *dialogue* refers to a process of endless redescriptions of the world by people with different beliefs and perspectives. Through dialogue, people develop mutual understanding that transforms how they see themselves and others. In this way, counseling is a dialogue between the client's structures and the structures of the social environment, where the caregiver may be understood as one of many elements in that environment.

IN PASSING

What clients learn in the course of counseling is how their actions are dependent upon the intellectual categories they use to define the significant elements in their worlds. Knowing that we know compels us to consider how we might live our lives differently. According to Maturana and Varela (1992), "it compels us to see that the world will be different only if we live differently. It compels us because, when we know that we know, we cannot deny (to ourselves or to others) that we know" (p. 245). Accepting that we are fully responsible for shaping our world, we may begin to accept the reality that if we created our world, then we have the power to change it.

NOTE

Adapted from R. L. Hayes. (1986). Human growth and development. In M. Lewis, R. L. Hayes, & J. Lewis (Eds.). *An introduction to the counseling profession* (pp. 36–95). Itasca, IL: F. E. Peacock. Republished with permission of the author; R. L. Hayes. (1991). Applications of interactionist developmental schemes to counseling theory and practice. In L. Kuhmerker, U. Gielen, & R. L. Hayes (Eds.), *The Kohlberg legacy for the helping professions* (pp. 188–200). Birmingham, AL: Religious Education Press. Republished with permission of Religious Education Press; R. L. Hayes.

(2001). Making meaning in groups: A constructivist developmental approach. In K. Fall & J. Levitov (Eds.), *Modern applications to group work* (pp. 263–280). Huntington, NY: Nova Science. Republished with permission of Nova Science Publishers, Inc.; R. L. Hayes. (2020). *Making meaning: A constructivist approach to counseling and groupwork in education*. Washington, DC: Lexington/Rowman & Littlefield. Republished with permission of Lexington/Rowman & Littlefield.

Chapter 4

Infants and Toddlers

If adults are to help children understand the losses they experience, they must understand the child's efforts to make meaning of those events. Critically, the focus should be on the child's own experience and the process of meaning-making. Through imitation and internalizing the cognitive processes provided by others, children can develop greater expertise and greater cultural understanding of loss. As explored in chapter 3, this process becomes a kind of *mediated learning experience* in which the interactions of the caregiver and the child "generate the capacity of individuals to change, to modify themselves in the direction of greater adaptability and toward the use of higher mental processes" (Feuerstein, 1979, p. 110). This approach helps to reveal the child's own understanding of the associated events. Particularly with younger children, it gives them permission to trust their own observations and judgments about the situation as part of an ongoing process of empowerment. Caregivers should listen to any questions and ask themselves what this tells them about the child's efforts to make sense of what has happened as well as any concerns about anticipated future losses.

Too often, well-meaning but protective adults view children as too delicate or too young to handle information about loss. This failure to openly validate the experience of loss and resultant grief can lead to *disenfranchised grief* (Doka, 2018) and the implication that the child has no right to grieve or a claim to social support. In this way, adults often succeed in insulating themselves from their own concerns about unresolved or anticipated events. This self-protective and misinformed approach often reflects the cumulative experience, or more properly the lack of experience, of the adult in dealing with similar issues. How we handle the greater disappointments of adulthood is influenced by our understanding of the "smaller" losses we experienced in childhood. If adults are to help children, it will be necessary to understand their own reactions to loss. And if they are to help children understand the losses they experience, adults must understand the child's efforts to make meaning of those events *as the child understands them.*

TWO MISUNDERSTANDINGS ABOUT CHILDREN

Psychologist David Elkind (1974) has written about some of the "self-evident assumptions" adults make about children which, upon reflection, turn out to be incorrect. "One of the most serious and pernicious misunderstandings about young children is that they are most like adults in their thinking and least like us in their feelings. In fact, just the reverse is true" (p. 51). Despite several decades of research on human development and its application to education, Elkind's conclusion remains as critically accurate today as it was a full two generations ago (McDevitt & Ormrod, 2019). This type of misunderstanding prompts parents to tell a 4-year-old child that "everything will be all right" while simultaneously encouraging the child to "stop that crying." Children who believe that the moon follows them when they walk will make little sense of an unhappy event that can somehow "make everything all right." By contrast, a caring spouse would not think of saying to her grieving partner that somehow things will be better if only he would stop crying. To be able to help children cope with the inevitable separations and losses they experience, adults must understand that children feel as we do in these circumstances, but they make a different sense of the events.

"A second misunderstanding about young children," Elkind (1974) explains, "is that they learn best while they are sitting still and listening" (p. 52). Certainly, adults do learn by sitting quietly and reflecting upon their actions or by listening to the shared wisdom of others. But for young children, the activity of learning is of a different kind than that of most adults. With children the idea of active learning must be taken quite literally. Children truly learn only by acting and experiencing the concrete effects of their actions.

Thus, the child who has lost a tricycle, had a pet die, or dropped a scoop of ice cream from the top of a cone must be helped to confront the loss directly. Adults who replace the tricycle, bring home a new pet, or offer another ice cream cone in consolation, without an intervening period (however brief) to allow the child to experience the full impact of the associated loss, deny the child a significant opportunity to learn about change and oneself. In contrast, helping the child to make better sense of the event and to experience the loss in its entirety does nothing less than stimulate development itself.

Advances in children's understanding of loss and related events represent increased cognitive capacity and variability of approaches for problem solving. Regular patterns of change in children's thinking about loss and related events can be conceptualized as falling into a series of overlapping periods. These periods represent general changes in the child's way of knowing, where each succeeding period represents a greater capacity of the child to make sense of a greater variety of experiences in a more adequate way.

THE BIRTH OF LOSS

In birth, newborns have their first encounters with death and experience first-hand the pain of separation that comes with change and loss. Consider what you might have learned about the world in this first encounter with it. You moved from a soft, warm, dark, quiet, totally nourishing place into a harsh sensory bombardment. You were physically abused, violated in numerous ways, and subjected to physical pain and insult, all of which could possibly be overcome if it weren't for one additional act of cruelty: You were isolated from your mother (Hendricks & Weinhold, 1982, p. 51).

Responding to calls for more humane childbirth practices (see Janov, 1970; Klaus & Kennell, 1976; Le Boyer, 1975; Pearce, 1977), greater attention was directed in the 1980s to the impact of the trauma of birth on the newborn. A review of contemporary childbirth practices, however, has revealed that the press for a change in such practices was less about a consideration of the impact of birth on the child and more about the woman's right to direct her own medical care supported by a burgeoning feminist movement (Behruzi et al., 2013). Today, we recognize that the meaning childbirth holds for the individual, like so many other significant life events, is socially constructed.

Differing cultural practices notwithstanding, these first days as a "stranger in a strange land" subject the infant to a succession of temporary separations and unanticipated reunions. They are "unanticipated" because the infant is essentially a sensory being, directing all activity toward the incorporation of objects to satisfy immediate needs. Lacking the cognitive sophistication to understand causality and finality, the child finds it difficult to understand loss as something permanent or that events have causes.

The child's reflexive behaviors, such as sucking and grasping, are generalized, strengthened, and differentiated. Because the child's interactions with the environment are characterized by *actions on objects* and involve sensory and motor movements, Piaget (1954/1936) referred to this as the *sensorimotor period* of development. Objects are assimilated into developing schemes of "things to suck," "things to grasp," and so forth. Evidence of the rudiments of sensorimotor thinking appears in adult life when people describe a spiral staircase by circling their fingers in the air, or when they open and close two fingers against one another while searching for a lost pair of scissors. Much of the nonverbal behavior or physiological symptoms experienced by clients who come to counseling are the expression of thoughts at a sensorimotor level.

Unaware of time and without a sense of self-improvement, infants pass through states of wakefulness and sleeping that appear no more predictable to them than the parade of faces that pass over the horizon of their cribs. Yet, in their playful explorations they begin to see a regularity in the events about them and in the parts they play in causing such events. When out of sight is out of existence, the child is fascinated anew each time Jack pops from his box or playful parents suddenly appear from behind closed hands in a game of peek-a-boo. A growing awareness of objects and events leads to new experiments and new understandings.

The objectification of things as separate from the self marks an intellectual revolution in the child's thinking. No longer content to wait for Jack to appear, the child now pulls at the lid to *make* Jack come out; peek-a-boo is replaced with hide-and-seek; unwanted foods are now thrown like missiles to the far reaches of the kitchen in nascent experiments in physics. The child's seeming self-absorption in an undifferentiated world is evolving toward an understanding of the world as consisting of objects from which to choose. This recognition of objects in the world signals the child's "emergence from embeddedness" (Schachtel, 1959) in a world heretofore unrecognized. In differentiating itself from the world, the child develops a sense of self independent of the world in which it recurringly finds itself. And by this transformation, the emerged self gives way to a new individualized self, apart from yet dependent upon the world that surrounds it.

The end of this period is marked by the beginnings of *representational thought* in which the child can think about an object that is not actually present. The child can now dream or search in several places for an object that has been hidden in different places in sequence. The development of the concept of *object permanence,* allows the child to recognize that objects continue to exist outside of the child's presence. Thus, the child now misses the primary caregiver who has until now come and gone without notice.

The concept of loss itself is born. What can now be found can now be lost. The infant, in emerging from embeddedness in sensorimotor activity can now relate to self and others as objects unto themselves. In so doing, however, the infant must give up the *me-that-went-before* in favor of a *new-me.* This repudiation involves the construction of meaning itself through an evolutionary process whereby objects are differentiated from the self and integrated with the self simultaneously. Thus, the process of differentiating the self from the objects of its experience creates the possibility for integrating the *self* with *other* and initiates the lifelong themes of discovery and loss.

The growing recognition that objects exist apart from the self ushers in a great new development in the child's relationship with others. Because the child begins to imagine caregivers in their absence, true loss is experienced intellectually for the first time. The loss of objects once known creates more than the visceral reaction to changing climatic conditions (e.g., diapering, feeding, washing). Differentiating *absent* from *present* gives rise to the universal experience of anxiety that accompanies separation from the primary caregiver (Bowlby, 1980). As argued above, this anxiety is the consequence of a failure to make sense of the perturbation that has disrupted present, until now, modes of thinking. The effort to make sense of the event, to state one's past, is a way of gaining control over the world and understanding its meaning for future conduct. The failure to find a precise meaning for this change of perspective and the inability to forecast a comprehensible future is the very definition of anxiety.

This transformation takes place over a period of roughly two to twenty-one months of age, during which the child experiments with the concept of permanent loss. Toilets are flushed repeatedly, objects are tossed from car windows, and parents swallow the child's unwanted food in demonstration of the "all-gone" phenomenon. Yet, the child's anxiety is not so much about the loss of an object or another as it is about the loss of the child's very organization. Allowed to explore the permanence of some objects and the permanent disappearance of others, children begin to develop the kind of healthy self that trusts in others' efforts to help. Trust helps the child feel secure in receiving support from others and encourages seeking out the opportunity in each crisis.

This analysis of the origins of the loss phenomenon may seem unnecessarily detailed and drawn out, but its significance lies as much in what it suggests about finding as it does about losing. The creation of objectivity involves the simultaneous loss of self as subject, but by the complimentary process the loss of oneself creates a new object. The not-me that was before is now differentiated from the new me, or even a future one, that replaces it. This re-creative cycle of lost and found underlies the basic process for the development of personality itself. To live life involves taking the risk to *be* alive. In daring to care for and about others, we run the risk of losing them and ourselves in the process. The other side of loss, however, is to discover new meaning for our lives and to re-create a new *self* out of this loss of the old self.

THE MAGIC YEARS

At just the point when objects wholly exist for the child (about 21 months), separation anxiety ceases to exist. The successful child has developed the kind of self that is separate from, though not wholly independent of, others. Early in this period, children begin to accept the idea of an "all-powerful force in the universe," which reflects their own egocentric understanding. The thinking of children in this period tends to concentrate on just one aspect of a situation or problem. Piaget referred to this thinking as *pre*-operational because the child does not *operate* on multiple aspects of a situation simultaneously. Because pre-operational children cannot distinguish between internal mental states and external reality, they fail to take another's point of view.

Unable to differentiate their own thoughts from those of others, toddlers find great difficulty in imagining things unlike themselves.

This period, which extends from approximately age two through seven, is marked by the development of the *symbolic function* of language. The child's interactions involve *actions on symbols*, which permit representational interactions. Teddy bears can carry on conversations and, most importantly, words can be used to create language. Children now learn the language of death and loss as they are introduced to the particular vocabulary of their family and culture.

> The car will not start because the battery is "done for." In a dart game, while "killing" time, someone threw one "dead" center. An exasperated parent yells to the children to "knock it off" after coming home "dead' tired from a day spent with "deadbeats" who are trying to "make a killing" in the market. A "wake" has been scheduled for a neighbor who recently "bought the farm." On the other hand, adult language tries to avoid the use of the words "dead" or "die" when death itself is actually spoken about. So, we "put pets to sleep" and people "pass on" or are "lost" or "expire" when we really mean they are "dead." No wonder children have trouble understanding what we are saying to them.

The outcomes of this period include the notion of cause-effect relationships and the understanding that an object has its own identity despite changes in its appearance. These children do not understand, however, that their personal reactions *are* reactions.

> Aaron came in from play one day to find his fish floating upside down at the top of the tank. Puzzled by this novel position, he asked his mom; "Why is Fenwick swimming upside down?"
>
> "He's not swimming," answered his mom uncomfortably. "He's dead. Fish do that when they die."
>
> "Do they like to lie that way when they're dead?" he asked.
>
> "I suppose so," answered his mom, somewhat at a loss for anything better to say.
>
> A month or so later, Aaron's playmate told him that his grandfather had died and that he had seen him lying asleep on his back in a large box. "Oh, he's not sleeping," Aaron explained. "Things like to lie that way when they're dead."

Building upon Piaget's stage theory, psychologist Maria Nagy (1948) developed her own stage theory of children's conceptions of death from her analysis of written compositions, drawings, and interviews with 378 Hungarian children. Based on this work, she found that children under age five regarded death as a reversible process, much as they jump up after a round of "Bang, bang—you're dead." For these children, death is a kind of life. As one four-year-old remarked, "After you die, you get buried, and then you have to stay there for the rest of your life." Objects, too, live on after death. For the child who believes that brooms can become horses, that wrecked cars get hurt, and that trees like to stand out in the rain, things that are lost miss us as much as we miss them.

> At age 3 or 4 while shopping with my mother, I overheard a conversation with a neighbor: "It's a shame she lost her mother. She was so young." I envisioned a girl my age walking out of a store, noticing her mother wasn't following, and not being able to find her. I asked my mother if the girl found her mother. I don't remember her answer, but it could not have been very comforting because for years I couldn't understand why the girl had stopped looking for her mother and how it was possible for them never to find each other.

Relying primarily on their excellent perceptual capabilities, the world for young children is something to be heard, seen, touched, tasted, and smelled. The physical properties of objects are undifferentiated from the child's subjective reaction to the object itself. Thus, divorce is perceived correctly as the parent moving away from the child. But the bad feelings associated with the loss of the parent are confused with *being bad.* Examples of pre-operational thought in adults include wishful or magical thinking, superstitious behavior, or the recurrent though illogical belief that our bad thoughts may have caused others harm. It is no wonder that statements that the child didn't *cause* the divorce make little sense at such times. Furthermore, the toddler's reliance upon physical cues in definition of self makes hospitalization and the possibility of death, or the loss of body parts or bodily functions, a particularly anxiety-laden situation.

MEDIATING IN LOSS

Because the experiential lives of infants are limited to what they can feel, touch, smell, taste, or hear, the losses they experience are bound to changes in their physical environment. Because infants have yet to develop language and can't tell us what they are thinking, caregivers are limited to behavioral clues. Although infants have yet to develop a concept of loss per se, any kind of change in the familiar, safe, or comfortable often manifests itself in the form of a grief reaction. Infants may become irritable and even hard to console, may cry more or variously be less responsive, may seem anxious, may experience some weight loss, or may appear to be searching for someone. Caregivers will need to be especially attuned to the "normal" behavior of the infant to be able to monitor any reactions to the loss of the familiar.

Infants can experience grief, particularly when they are grieving a primary caregiver. Premature babies who have spent extended periods in the hospital prior to coming home, newly adopted infants, or an infant whose primary caregiver has died or returned to work after a pregnancy leave will all experience some loss. The infant who has been so dependent on the caregiver in meeting his or her needs, who has experienced the caregiver's touch through being held, fed, diapered, and bathed is gone. So too is the routine of waking and sleeping, being touched in a special way, along with the ambient smells, soothing sounds, and the sight of the caregiver's face. The demands on any new caregiver may be the same, but how, when, where, and in what form the infant's demands are met will not be the same.

Until each has learned the routine of the other, the infant will continue to experience the loss of the original caregiver. The experience of each loss is likely to be recursive as infant and caregiver adjust to living with one another. In helping infants gain some mastery over the objects they are coming to know as independent from themselves, the best thing you can do as a caregiver is to maintain routines. And, in the face of loss, increase physical contact to reassure the infant's sense of safety and reduce the anxiety that accompanies the fear of being abandoned. With repeated experience in understanding and recognizing the infant's behavior and appropriately meeting the infant's needs, there will be a growing trust in the reliability of the caregiver. And with trust comes the possibility hope brings in imagining a safe and comfortable future.

As crawling gives way to walking, the infant grows into a toddler whose world expands with each step. Encounters with new objects bring new understandings while exploration results in the setting of new boundaries. Unable to differentiate their own thoughts from external reality, each change offers the possibility they too will be lost. Increasing facility in the use of language to order their world provides a new vehicle for helping the toddler to make meaning of any loss. In discussing loss with children during this period, one must ask for the child's understanding and gear explanations to the child's own experience. Focusing on the intent of the child's question rather than its literal content may help in understanding the nature of the child's loss. Supportive comments should address the child's magical ("if only . . . ") thinking with a balance of factual information: "I wish we could see our old friends today, too, but we live far away in a new neighborhood now and need to make new friends here."

Start with short, simple, and truthful explanations geared to the toddler's level of understanding. Break explanations into manageable parts and wait for any additional questions. Because toddlers tend to concentrate on a single aspect of any loss, they are likely to overinterpret its meaning for themselves. The death of another opens the possibility for their own death. Acknowledge their fear but offer reassurance that you are there to protect them. Help them to understand that everyone gets sick at some time, but not everyone dies. "I am here to take care of you even when you get sick."

Toddlers who witness any loss due to an accident or breakage, for instance, need to be reassured that things do break and people do get hurt but that is why we are careful. Toddlers may act out their thinking in their play as they recreate accidents with their toys or break things only to see if they can be put back together. Talking out loud as they reenact these events gives them some mastery over the loss and helps to ensure confidence in their abilities to handle similar situations. Wheat and Whiting (2018) caution that "the imagination, magical thinking, and fantasy common in early childhood leave children vulnerable to inaccurate and sometimes harmful ideas about their loss that is harmful if left uncorrected" (p. 96). The clear message to give children is that the event is not their fault, that they were not bad or unlovable, and that there is nothing they could have done to make things different.

Rehearsing the circumstances of the loss serves to reinforce its permanence. Children who delight in hearing the same story repeated night after night demand the same predictability in understanding the losses that take them by surprise. Just as toddlers enjoy hearing the same story read to them over and over, they may continue to ask the same questions about any loss. This rehearsal helps in part to fully understand the loss and, in part, to reassure themselves that the outcome remains the same. In this way, bibliotherapy can be quite effective in helping toddlers to expand their vocabulary about a particular loss and thereby expand their capacity for making meaning of any loss in general. As well, give toddlers creative ways to express their feelings through drawing, or writing, or playing games. Such activities expand the range of options for making sense of any loss and help promote mastery over change in the future.

Finally, as much as possible, maintain existing rules and limits. Relaxing the consequences for any "bad" behavior may ease your pain, but toddlers need to know what did and didn't change to feel secure in the face of loss. Unable to accommodate the experience of others into their own thinking, these children adamantly defend the assertion that "It won't happen to me." Rather than argue with children about whether to take a favorite toy on a trip "because it might get lost," parents might suggest that Pooh Bear might like to "stay home with his family since you are going off with yours."

IN PASSING

If change and loss are inevitable, and if the experience associated with loss is related to the development of one's capacity to make sense of that change, young people need to know about the changes that can affect their lives. As asserted in previous chapters, *development is essentially the task of mastering the facts of one's existence.* As complex as this process may appear to adults, consider how thoroughly bewildering loss must be to the minds of children not yet sure who they are themselves. As caregivers, we must do more for young people than help them acknowledge their pain. We have an obligation to help them understand their feelings and how they are involved in creating them. The challenge is to help them face life directly. Meeting this challenge means helping them to understand change and to make better choices in the face of it. Helping children make better choices involves helping them acknowledge loss rather than fight against it and necessitates increasing their responsiveness to change.

NOTE

Adapted from R. L. Hayes. (1986). Human growth and development. In M. Lewis, R. L. Hayes, & J. Lewis (Eds.). *An introduction to the counseling profession* (pp. 36–95). Itasca, IL: F. E. Peacock. Republished with permission of the author; R. L. Hayes. (2020). *Making meaning: A constructivist approach to counseling and group-work in education.* Washington, DC: Lexington/Rowman & Littlefield. Republished with permission of Lexington/Rowman & Littlefield.

Chapter 5

Middle Childhood

Middle childhood is initiated by a profound revolution in the child's development. Between the ages of five and seven, children experience significant physical, social, emotional, and cognitive changes. During this period, for example, the ability of children to plan their actions *before* drawing a simple picture emerges. Similarly, they develop the ability to tell "left" from "right" at about the same time. In an example more obviously related to loss, pre-school children hold magical beliefs about death, including its reversibility. Older children, on the other hand, believe that death is permanent, yet understand that not all things die.

Although psychologists continue to debate the reasons for this "five-to-seven shift," most of them note the newfound use of language to control their own behavior and to influence others. Recall from the previous chapter that language is born of loss and the infant's efforts at control. Similarly, changes in the language of the older child forecast the emergence of a new language prompted by efforts to control a changing world brought on by new understandings. These developmental advances demand both an increasing capacity to communicate with others and a widening perspective of the child's sense of self in relationship to others. New cognitive capacities and an ever-increasing sophistication in the use of language introduces these children to a new world filled with wonder. It will also be a world filled with new forms of loss.

What events could account for such changes? As you might expect, developmental psychologists are divided in their interpretations. Some point to increasing differentiation and specialization of the nervous system, while others point to changing social opportunities created by widening participation in the family, with friends, and with people in the community and school. Still others argue for the child's growing capacity to take the perspective of others. Whatever the specific causes, the children who emerge on the other side of this shift make meaning of their experience in a way that is profoundly different from their earlier method.

A SHIFT IN PERSPECTIVE

Despite how apparent these changes are to the trained eye of the professional, parents are often unaware of such changes. Instead, they may treat each incident as an isolated event or attribute the novel behavior to new or unusual circumstances. Consider the following exchange between two siblings:

> Eight-year-old Shandra approached her mother and five-year-old brother Willy while the two sat contentedly on lounge chairs playing checkers near the family pool. Eyeing a bag of potato chips lying near her brother, Shandra asked: "Let me have some of those chips, will ya?"
>
> "No," came Willy's quick but casual reply. Startled by the response, Shandra persisted: "Come on; please?"
>
> "No!" replied Willy, a bit more assertively. "They're mine!"
>
> "What's your point?" asked Shandra, a bit indignant that her little brother would dare to refuse her. "Didn't I give you some of mine yesterday?" she offered, hoping now to have persuaded her brother by her appeal to the implicit quid pro quo in their exchange.
>
> "So?" came Willy's retort. "What's the deal?"
>
> "The deal . . . " began Shandra, deliberately choosing her words, "the deal is that I gave you some of my chips and now you owe me." Pausing to consider her own argument momentarily, she added, just for emphasis: "That's the way it works."
>
> "Oh, Shandra!" interrupted their mother, her voice betraying some mild irritation with the discussion. "Can't you see we're playing a game here? Be a bit more considerate," she offered. Then, more as an order than a request, she concluded, "Go inside and get something else for yourself."
>
> "But, Mom," Shandra whined, "it's just not fair that he gets to keep them all for himself." And, pressing to the heart of the issue for herself, she added, "How come I have to lose all the time and he gets to win?"

To understand this exchange as something more than just a petty quarrel between siblings, the mother would need to be aware of the important differences in the ways the two children understand this event. Aside from the interruption and her mother's personal irritation with her demands, Shandra has a more complex understanding of the situation than Willy. For him, giving in to his sister's demands would mean a loss of control over the snacks without any apparent gain. For Shandra, the issue had become more than access to a snack, but rather her rightful share in the exchange of goods as part of a larger set of interpersonal expectations. Hers was not the loss of something to eat. Rather, she lost faith in the importance of being a good person, something neither her brother nor her mother seemed to appreciate. Of course, this latest revolution in Shandra's thinking did not happen overnight. And Willy is unlikely to continue to think as he does now. But for the mother's part, she failed to recognize the developmental significance of the event that unfolded before her.

COORDINATION AND CONSERVATION

The major cognitive task for school-age children is the mastery of classes, quantities, and relations. Typically, by the age of seven or eight, children move on from the magical thinking of the pre-school years to the kind of thinking Piaget (1954/1936) called *concrete operational.* Its distinguishing feature, and hence its name, is the development of operational thought. An *operation* is an internalized action that is part of an organized structure. Interactions during this period involve *operations upon objects.* Just as the preschool child evolved from the infant who could not differentiate self from other, so the primary school child evolves from the pre-school child who cannot differentiate self from perception. The child no longer *is* his or her perceptions, but rather *has* perceptions. The school-age child can now coordinate perceptions in a reversible cognitive movement. The child can now hold onto two thoughts at the same time, thus allowing for the comparison of one object to another, one event to another, one experience to another. Moreover, the child can now compare the outcome of past behavior with present conditions. The experience of loss now has a new ally. Life as known can now be compared to life as experienced and the congruity or incongruity between the two measured and necessary adjustments made.

This movement back and forth between perceptions allows the child to construct groups and classes of objects and to make a changing world stand still—to make it concrete. These children can be expected to consider options in advance. They have become more self-conscious in their behavior; in effect, they have a conscience. It is now possible to compare what one should have done, and didn't and conversely, what one didn't do with what one did. This developmental advance permits these children to establish truly reciprocal relationships and, in turn, to experience the loss that comes when others fail to live up to the child's expectations.

During this period, more mature forms of role-taking emerge by which the thoughts and intentions of others are considered. Thought is now decentered, dynamic, and reversible. Individuals who are concrete operational thinkers can appreciate lawful nature in the events of the world, which is now in equilibrium with their own system of logic. Just as each new stage is liberating, however, it is also limiting. Thinking in this period can only be applied to concrete objects that are either mentally or physically present. In effect, the thinking of this period is bound to the concrete reality of what *is* rather than to the abstract reality of what *could be.*

In a complimentary way, the child begins to appreciate the identity of an object is conserved despite apparent changes in its appearance. A pie is the same size, no matter how many pieces you cut it into; a game is won or lost using the same rules no matter where you play it; and your mother and father are still your parents even if they divorce one another. In their efforts to make meaning of the world they are only beginning to understand, these children begin to think systematically about the social as well as the physical properties of that world.

In a new egocentrism that does not distinguish between fact and assumption, these children are thoroughly engaged in an exploration of the limits of the physical world. The development of operational thought permits the child to seriate objects or events in their proper order, such as small to large or first to last. The child also begins to understand part-whole relationships, as in bigger or smaller. The newfound capacity to order things in classes is acted out in building collections and sorting things that belong to *either* X *or* Y. This either/or thinking creates their familiar interest in the good guys and bad guys, right and wrong behavior, or the establishment of clubs to separate the "in" group from the "out" group. Building a clubhouse does more than put concrete physical boundaries around those like oneself, however; it helps children gain a measure of control over their world. Of course, if things can be included, then they can also be excluded or missing. A clubhouse also protects the child from the loss that isolation would bring. The ability to create classes of objects introduces the possibility of losing things that the child doesn't yet have. Hopes, dreams, and the "best laid plan" can be lost with all the force of losing "real" objects.

The rule-building behavior of children at this point in their development is well-established (Cobb-Moore et al., 2016). So much of the behavior of concrete operational children is devoted to *filling in the boxes* of life, making predictions, ordering classes of objects, and drawing comparisons. Their inability to differentiate hypothesis from fact, however, results in their failure to understand fully that the rules are of their own making. It should come as no surprise, therefore, that the primary sources of loss for school-age children lie in the failure of others to live by what they understand to be the "rules of the game."

A NEW EGOCENTRISM

The inability of school-age children to differentiate hypothesis from fact results in their failure to understand fully that they are the ones who made up many of the rules for governing other people's behavior. These children are embedded in their own concreteness. They operate from a new egocentrism that does not distinguish between fact and assumption. Shandra, for example, failed to realize that her assumptions about what would be right and fair are not necessarily shared by either her brother or her mother.

Instead, these children operate on what Elkind (1974) has called assumptive realities, "assumptions about reality that children make on the basis of limited information and which they will not alter in the face of new and contradictory evidence" (p. 79). In a sense, these children are compelled by the force of their own logic. In Shandra's case, she failed to anticipate that her own ethic about sharing, however logical it appeared to her, would not also be shared by her brother. Further, in the face of her brother's repeated refusal to share, she remained steadfast in her interpretation that "That's the way it works." Her assumptions that her mother would appreciate her position and might support it were equally disappointing. It's not surprising, therefore, to find that primary school children are easily and constantly disappointed when what they had hoped would come true doesn't. Their lives, which are made up of so much wishing and hoping, are acted out in the face of recurring disappointment and loss. Unaware of their own part in the drama, these children are often surprised when they meet the future they worked so hard to forecast.

My father used to tell the story of a time when his grade school class was having a costume party: "I had the makings of a pirate costume because some way or another I owned a genuine rubber dagger. This, then, got me to dress with a bandana on my head, eye patch, torn shorts, open neck shirt, and real pirate boots. The boots were galoshes with the tops folded down so they almost covered the buckles. Into the right-hand boot was thrust my 8-inch rubber dagger. This was the focal point of the entire ensemble. I would be the best of the group—a real swashbuckler. I would be able to slash and stab with my rubber dagger, scare some of my classmates, and be the envy of the rest. Off I trudged to school, and the party soon was in full swing. I reached for my dagger. It was gone! I had lost it on the way. I had nothing to fall back on, no alternate plan. I was completely abashed, devastated, and probably sulked on the sidelines. I never did find the dagger, which, as far as I know, is still somewhere between home and school."

This example provides a rich array of assumptive realities: that others would share in the illusion of a pirate created by his costume, that they would consequently be frightened by the dagger (which was no longer merely rubber but now a pirate's dagger), and that the pirate would be the envy of all at the party. And a final assumptive reality is that without the dagger, the ensemble was incomplete, the classmates would no longer fear the pirate, and thus he would not be the envy of his classmates. If the dagger is lost, then all is lost, and the illusion of a powerful and envied self is lost as well.

Such a constellation of assumptive realities leads children to over-rely upon their own assessment of the situation and to underestimate the contributions of others. If, as the concrete operational child assumes, the world is an orderly place, that is governed by rules, and these rules can be known, then games are not just to be played, but they are to be won or lost. This condition is especially true when they play children's games with adults. Winning confirms the child's reality, while losing challenges it. To maintain the set of assumptive realities, the child exaggerates the importance of confirmatory evidence and minimizes or even denies evidence to the contrary. Winning is evidence of a "great victory" while losing is "no big deal." Losing the game challenges the child's whole set of coordinated assumptions and threatens to disrupt the "real" world as the child knows it. When an adult is involved in the loss, regaining the child's trust is particularly important.

Ten-year-old Benjamin showed great improvement in his schoolwork despite his mother's concerns that he might do poorly following her recent separation from his father. In addition, his behavior at home had improved: he kept his room picked up without her having to nag him; his fights with his younger sister had all but disappeared; and bedtime came and went each evening without the customary outbursts that had characterized the previous few months. Contrary to her expectations that he would be distraught, he appeared downright happy.

There were some small difficulties: he continued to refer to his father's absence as a "business trip" despite his mother's equally persistent corrections that his father was living in town. Each evening whenever the phone rang, he would rush to answer it saying, "Oh, it's probably Dad calling from Santiago (or some other distant locale). I guess he won't be able to come home tonight." And despite the absence of Dad's chair from the living room, he would walk around the spot where it had been, being ever so careful not to "bump into it." "I'd better sit on the couch," he would say. "Dad will want to sit in his chair to watch the news when he gets home later."

Six weeks had passed when the counselor called to say he had been involved in a fight at school. Apparently, he had been working quietly at his desk when a classmate asked him innocently if he would be attending the upcoming school picnic. "What picnic?" he asked.

"What are you? Stupid?" came his classmate's incredulous reply. "The father-son picnic," his classmate explained. "Everybody's goin'!"

And with the words hardly spoken, Benjamin slammed his fist into his classmate's face, challenging him "to take it back!"

Neither he nor his mother spoke as they took the long ride home from school. "You go in the house and wash up," she said as they pulled up to the house.

"I'll do whatever I want. You're not the boss of me!" he shouted as he slammed the car door shut and trudged for the house. Through the door he went, throwing his books to the floor, then his hat, his gloves, and his coat. And then with one final, furious blast, he threw himself into his father's "chair" only to land so hard that he hurt himself. "Damn floor! Damn chair! Damn him!" he shouted. And realizing what he'd said, sat and wept as much now for the hurt by a father, as well as a chair, that wasn't there to support him when he needed it.

Clinicians might remark that Benjamin was in denial, noting that he was holding on to a view of the world that was contradicted by the "facts." But his assumptive reality about his father's goodness sustained him in his belief about his own goodness. By upholding the father's "good intentions" to be home despite his work schedule, Benjamin could uphold his own set of assumptions about the whole constellation of beliefs he had constructed through a lifetime of direct experience with a supportive father. To doubt his father would be to doubt himself and violate the "rules of the game" of relationships—rules he was unaware that he himself had created. Further, by being a "good boy" himself, he could preserve his relationship with his mother and sister in the absence of his father.

Only when his father failed him, in the context of the challenge by his peer, was he forced to choose between two competing and uncoordinated realities. By striking out at his classmate, he could be "good," as the benevolent defender of his father, *and* dramatically demonstrate that he is "bad" enough to be deserving of having been abandoned by his father. With one blow, he was able to "win" both games despite the losses to be realized in doing so.

Perhaps the most important development of this period is *conservation,* the ability to maintain relationships between objects despite their physical manipulation. The child who believed during the previous period that a pizza cut into eight pieces was larger than one cut only into six, now understands that cutting does not change the amount of pizza; it only changes the number and size of the pieces. The ability to conserve permits the child to perceive a certain stability about the world and to make plans for the future. Plans, once made however, can also be canceled, issuing in much of the disappointments experienced during this period as futures once imagined are lost. Author L. M. Montgomery has beautifully captured this theme in her portrayal of the eleven-year-old orphan Anne Shirley in her book *Anne of Green Gables*.

As Anne contemplates the events of the day ahead, she shares her thoughts with her guardian, Marilla: "I don't feel that I could endure the disappointment if anything happened to prevent me from getting to the picnic. I suppose I'd live through it, but I'm certain it would be a lifelong sorrow. It wouldn't matter if I got to a hundred picnics in after years; they wouldn't make up for missing this one. They're going to have boats on the Lake of Shining Waters—and ice cream, as I told you. I have never tasted ice cream. [Her close friend] Diana tried to explain what it was like, but I guess ice cream is one of those things that are beyond the imagination."

On Sunday Anne confided to Marilla on the way home from church that she grew actually cold all over with excitement when the minister announced the picnic from the pulpit. "Such a thrill as went up my back, Marilla! I don't think I'd ever actually believed until then that there was honestly going to be a picnic. I couldn't help fearing I'd only imagined it. But when a minister says a thing in the pulpit you just have to believe it."

"You set your heart too much on things, Anne," said Marilla, with a sigh. "I'm afraid there'll be a great many disappointments in store for you through life."

"Oh, Marilla, looking forward to things is half the pleasure of them!" exclaimed Anne. "You mayn't get the things themselves; but nothing can prevent you from having the fun of looking forward to them. [Marilla's friend] Mrs. Lynde says, 'Blessed are they who expect nothing for they shall not be disappointed.' But I think it would be worse to expect nothing than to be disappointed." (Montgomery, 1908, XIII, p. 3)

Such is the nature of hope: the belief in a better future. To hope is not merely to wish, but rather to believe in a realizable future. Unaware of her own role in the construction of that future, Anne's hope becomes reality when affirmed by a trusted authority. Hoping also serves as an act of defiance against the pessimism of Marilla and Mrs. Lynde. In this way, Anne both preserves the self that hopes while constructing a future into which to grow.

MAINTAINING CONTROL

Faced with a world in which disappointment lurks behind every assumption, primary school children come to rely upon their keen powers of observation. In her study of Hungarian children, Nagy (1948) found they were likely to personify death, seeing it as an angel or as an old man. Understanding that death is permanent, a fact confirmed by their perceptions, primary school children can nonetheless gain a measure of control over it through objectifying it. This insight helps to explain the great interest in stories about ghosts, wizards, vampires, angels, alternative worlds, and transcending terminal illness that children show during this period. Although unable to confirm Nagy's findings in his studies with children in the United States, Koocher (1973) found that they used specific details such as stereotyped accounts of what would happen rather than personification "as a means to mastery and hence 'control' over death" (p. 375).

Near the end of this period, children come to accept the permanency of death and the reality of loss *as a part of* the natural order of things. Unable to accept that death can come to anyone at any age, they believe that losses are governed by some set of rules: people die when they get old; automobiles fall apart after 10 years or 100,000 miles, whichever comes first; students fail when teachers don't like them; and food is spoiled when it reaches its expiration date.

Recall from chapter 1 that anxiety arises in efforts to control anticipated loss. We worry about losing control over events that are important to us and that we believe may turn out other than desired. Not surprisingly, the things that worry children are developmentally related. Objects that children fear seem to appear at about the same age for many children, across different cultures, only to be replaced by other objects later in life. Through the age of two, the sensorimotor child tends to fear unpredictable environmental stimuli (e.g., slamming doors, barking dogs). With the advent of preoperational thought, children are capable of worrying in the sense that they can anticipate loss. Characteristically, they tend to worry about imagined events rather than being surprised by environmental stimuli. Most of the fears of three to six-year-old children are unrealistic, like attacks by exotic animals or imaginary creatures like ghosts, witches, and monsters. The child who first encounters going to school may be expected to exhibit some anxiety. Among other things, help the child cope with the fear of losing the caregiver who the child believes "has been left at home all alone."

In middle childhood, fantasy fears are replaced by more realistic concerns that relate to everyday life. Monsters under the bed are not real but crime, war, and someone-who-may-hurt-you are. Grounded in the reality of their own lives or vicariously through social media, the specter of war, bullying, child abuse, a global pandemic, and drive-by shootings are all quite real for these children.

(RE)GAINING CONTROL

The pre-school child often greets loss with a startled expression, crying, or assuming a flight posture. The primary school child, on the other hand, cries little, tending to challenge or understand the event instead. Attempts at mastery more often take verbal rather than physical forms as experience helps these children expand their negotiation skills. Anyone who has ever been the caregiver for a school-age child has had the experience of being told "You are not the boss of me." Understanding this "defiance" as an effort to regain control may help to avoid the potential confrontation between adult and child over who is "really" in charge. Over the course of the primary school years, these children gain increasing fluency in the use of language to mediate their own experience. The use in grammar of "like," "because," "unless," and "and so on" are advanced by the coordination of multiple meanings. While improving their negotiation skills with adults, and especially peers, they learn to use language to regulate, if not entirely control, the reactions of others. Insulting one's peers is raised to a fine art as calling another a "baby," "retard," "wimp," insulting your mother ("Yo Mama is so _____") or denigrating another's body ("She's so ugly that _____") all serve to protect a fragile but growing sense of self from the loss that can arise from the imagined rejection by one's peers.

MEDIATING IN LOSS

In working with primary school children, one must recognize their great need for order and control. This means being completely (not necessarily fully) honest and accurate. Adults who don't know answers to these children's questions should say they don't know and encourage children to share their own thoughts and feelings. Caregivers should attempt to understand the child's loss and recognize that it is the size of the hurt that is the measure of the child's loss.

A child's sense of order is disrupted by loss, and reactions can be overgeneralized to include any and all situations. Children in this stage often abandon an entire collection after the loss of a single piece, or they withdraw from those who love them following a loss. Simply changing family plans to go on a special outing, mom changing her work hours, or dad shaving his beard can be as disrupting initially to these children as death or divorce. To help the child isolate the event and to begin to restore the child's trust, one must be factual and reliable. Tell children what else, if anything, will change, and how long and in what capacity you will continue to be around. Keep all appointments, and be prompt, minimizing immediate, future losses when possible. Make statements that apply concretely to the child's own experience, avoiding abstractions or generalities ("I know I said we'd go to the game today, but I also have a responsibility to complete my work at the office. Remember when your team rescheduled its games? Our family had to change its plans suddenly then. Let's figure out together when we will be able to go").

As the child's repertoire of ways for dealing with loss increases, so too the child becomes aware of the boundaries set by others, especially adults. Ironically, as they grow in their resentment of the demands placed upon them for control, they become increasingly demanding of themselves. Children need to come to the realization that there are areas of their lives over which they have no choice. A planned family move to Tucson, or both parents working, or big sister getting married are issues beyond their control. Still, learning how to protect oneself from bullies, or how to use a telephone when home alone in an emergency, or how to ask for help when lost in a shopping mall help the child to become more competent.

As children's experience with loss grows, there is an increasing awareness of their own values. With increasing awareness come enhanced abilities to discuss what is important and, thereby, what has been lost. Believing that old patterns of responding to loss are outmoded, outdated, or just "kid stuff," they will begin to experiment with new and more socially appropriate ways of handling new losses. Because the child's first efforts to deal with loss in a new way are likely to be clumsy at best, it is important for caregivers to focus on the purpose of the child's often disruptive behavior as a means for dealing with disappointment and the possibility of further loss.

Increased experience in dealing with others, especially peers, will help these children gain greater impulse control. In time, they will place greater emphasis on meeting the group's expectations even if they don't understand that such expectations are assumptive realities of their own making. Through scaffolding (see Vygotsky as adapted by Wood et al., 1976), older siblings and the peer group can model effective ways to deal with loss within the confines of the rules of the game. Encouraging older siblings to help interpret the child's reaction can be especially helpful in creating new and more effective ways to deal with loss.

As well, bibliotherapy can provide excellent outlets for the vicarious expression of unresolved or unarticulated losses. Focusing on the motives and personalities of others helps these children to consider their own motives more carefully while also protecting them from criticism by adults or insensitive peers. In reading about others' attempts to overcome the challenges in their own lives, children gain increased empathy for others as they increase their capacity for role-taking. As well, they come to appreciate, by comparison, the present limits of their own strengths and weaknesses. Autobiographies help children to understand they are not alone in their fears. By normalizing the meaning they make of their experience, they can gain the courage to imagine a better future, which is the essence of hope. The life stories of other children and significant adults provide indirect experience with loss and death in a way that increases the child's understanding while limiting direct experience with the events themselves.

Caregivers are encouraged to use games and other rule-oriented activities to help primary school children to express their associated thoughts and feelings related to specific losses. Interaction with peers in structured games as a part of groupwork helps them to assess their own capabilities, gain greater empathy, and begin to exercise some social control. The use of imaginative play permits the child to practice basic cognitive skills within a safe environment that allows freedom of expression. Because the concrete operational child learns through operations on objects, play therapy permits the child a safe medium for the expression of ideas the child doesn't understand yet. Lacking a vocabulary sufficient to express ideas fully, the child may gain greater insight regarding particular losses through metaphor. The use of metaphor encourages the child's creativity in dealing with loss and provides a safe and controllable distance from which to negotiate the loss. Because we can never actually communicate our experience of loss directly, the use of metaphor allows us to share how we make meaning of the event in a form that others may understand. With the child's increasing capacity to create relationships between events, caregivers are encouraged to discuss anticipated losses to help the child plan more effectively.

Because grief is an ongoing process, losses experienced early in childhood must be reexamined and understood anew at succeeding stages of development. Old misunderstandings and confusions demand new interpretations. Anniversaries, holidays, familiar situations, and the restructuring of families give rise to old feelings (McCabe, 2003). For this reason, adults should examine their own ideas about death to avoid confusing young people with their own unresolved issues related to loss. This is particularly important in dealing with those losses that are personally distasteful, such as the loss of a caregiver through abuse, incest, mental illness, imprisonment, or suicide (Harris, 2011; Larson, 1993; Wheat & Whiting, 2018; Worden, 2018). Above all, recognize that the loss is being constructed within the developmental understanding of a child. This construction sets the pattern for developing a vocabulary and set of effective coping mechanisms for dealing with loss. How adults help children to deal with the little losses helps them develop the trust necessary to work through the bigger losses that loom ahead.

IN PASSING

As we have seen in this chapter, the era of middle childhood is ushered in by a dramatic transformation. The magical thinking of early childhood gradually gives way to a more reciprocal kind of thinking that permits the child to consider multiple possibilities simultaneously. With new understandings come new problems, however, as an ever-widening world demands an ever-broader perspective. Language takes on new forms in the child's efforts to exercise permanent control over continuous change. With each new experience, new losses give rise to new opportunities, and the ongoing challenge to relearn the world anew.

How adults help children to deal with the little losses helps them to develop the trust in others and in themselves that will be necessary to work through the outgrown child that each leaves behind. Learning to live with loss helps young people develop the courage to become the adult who lies ahead. In the next chapter we will see how the concrete world of middle childhood is challenged by yet another advance in the child's thinking. The changes brought on by this intellectual revolution challenge the adolescent to re-invent the self of childhood. How the adolescent negotiates the losses brought on by these changes in the reconstruction of a more reflective self is the focus of the next chapter.

NOTE

Adapted from R. L. Hayes. (1986). Human growth and development. In M. Lewis, R. L. Hayes, & J. Lewis (Eds.), *An introduction to the counseling profession* (pp. 36–95). Itasca, IL: F. E. Peacock. Republished with permission of the author; R. L. Hayes. (2020). *Making meaning: A constructivist approach to counseling and group-work in education.* Washington, DC: Lexington/Rowman & Littlefield. Republished with permission of Lexington/Rowman & Littlefield.

Chapter 6

Adolescents and Youth

Unlike the concrete operational children of the elementary school years, adolescents can differentiate fact from hypothesis. During this period, thought becomes truly logical. As adolescents grow in their capacity to consider the full range of dimensions to a problem, reality is recognized as one of many alternatives. Possibilities are considered alongside realities as the adolescent considers what *may be,* no longer limited to what *is.* Thinking involves *operations on symbols* and thus is concerned with the form of thought itself. This *formal operational thought* permits adolescents to exhibit true abstract thought and a systematic approach to problem solving. As with previous developmental advances, new ways of thinking introduce myriad new forms of loss that demand new problem-solving capacities.

Beginning as early as age nine, for some, and as late as age 16 for most, children in the United States begin to develop the capacity to reflect on their own thinking. Although full formal operations may represent a developmental advancement achieved by less than half of American adults, few adolescents or adults use concrete operational thought exclusively. Instead, they are more likely to use a combination of logical operations switching between them as the complexity of the problem demands.

My classmates and I had been asked to consider a "thought problem" by our junior high school science teacher. The very idea of a thought as a problem seemed intriguing enough. But then came the problem: "to consider what your tongue does all day. Not just when you're thinking about it, like right now, but all day, every day. What is your tongue doing in your mouth when you aren't paying attention to it?"

I'd never thought about it really. The problem seemed so simple at first. It just lies there waiting for me to give it something to do like lick, or suck, or talk. Yet the more I thought on the problem, the more I wondered how it was exactly that I knew what to tell it to do. And I wondered about the times that it did things I hadn't told it to do. How at times I bit it by mistake, or I got "tongue-tied," or it just said things that came out sounding stupid like "my zipper's down" when

71

I meant to say, "Mississippi town," or how it would suddenly screech out of control when least expected.

I began to wonder if maybe I had other body parts that were doing things without my permission. Sure enough, I found hair growing where it hadn't been. And then I became aware of thoughts I hadn't thought, and of songs that played on in my head for hours. An idea that had seemed so simple at first, now took up hours of my day in contemplation. I became acutely aware that things were going on in and around me all the time, without my knowledge, and most especially without my permission. "How long had things been going on like this?" "How much had I missed already?" I wondered would I ever be able to catch up and would I ever have it all under control again!

Because so much of adolescence is spent in anticipating the reaction of others in social situations, the adolescent is continually constructing, or reacting to what Elkind (1974) calls *an imaginary audience.* "It is an audience because the adolescent believes that he will be the focus of attention, and it is imaginary because, in actual social situations, this is not usually the case" (p. 91). Consider Storr's (2018) description of the narcissistic self-obsession with personal perfection of today's "selfie" generation and one has a reliable characterization of the interpersonal challenges faced by adolescents.

Convinced of others' interest in and scrutiny of them in the context of loss, adolescents react more with shame for who they are than with guilt for what they've done. Anticipating the reactions of others to their loss, adolescents wonder more about how they will look to others following a loss than about the loss per se (Hauser, 1983; Oltjenbruns, 2001). Unlike the preschooler's fear of dismemberment that accompanies hospitalization, surgery during adolescence raises the possibility of disfigurement and rejection by one's peers. In divorce, adolescents appear preoccupied with the inevitable embarrassment that will accompany the public discovery of their parents' conflict. The hypothesis rather than the fact is what is lost in adolescence. A young man who fails his driving test or young woman who places second in the track meet, as examples, mourn the loss of the admiration they anticipated from their friends. The victory celebrations, the congratulations in school hallways, and the adoring crowds asking to see the *trophy,* be it a driver's license or a medal, are all lost now.

Handguns, which were used to "tame" the West at the beginning of the previous century, are being used by adolescents today to kill one another in a limited understanding of personal freedom. In his analysis of school rampage shootings, for example, Larkin (2009) concluded that the Columbine High School shooting in 1999 "raised rampage shootings in the public consciousness from mere revenge to a political act" (p. 1320). Larkin argues that shooters Klebold and Harris, in their spectacular assault on Columbine High School, gave voice to outsiders, to loser students, to those left out of the mainstream, to the victims of jock and "prep" predation. To such a student, payback consists of killing convenient targets, making a statement, and dying in a blaze of glory. (pp. 1322–1323)

In a world where news has become entertainment, making a statement by killing one's classmates can lead to notoriety even if it comes at the cost of one's own life.

As Elkind (1974) offered: "One of the most common admiring audience constructions in the adolescent is the anticipation of how others will react to his own death. A certain bittersweet pleasure is derived from anticipating the belated recognition of his good qualities" (p. 92). Such is the poignant tale told by Mark Twain (1876) of Huck Finn's pride while observing his own funeral and that of his two friends presumed to have died. Equally engaging is Twain's description of the reactions of Huck's peers:

Then there was a dispute about who saw the dead boys last in life, and many claimed that dismal distinction, and offered evidences, more or less tampered with by the witness; and when it was ultimately decided who *did* see the departed last, and exchanged the last words with them, the lucky parties took upon themselves a sort of sacred importance, and were gaped at and envied by all the rest. (p. 145; emphasis in original)

Not surprisingly, adolescents are ambivalent about death, seeing in it the end of a physical world but the beginning of a better, more spiritual world. The anxiety this ambivalence provokes often develops into defiance, which is evident in the risk-taking behavior so characteristic of adolescents. The longstanding appeal of death for adolescents is reflected most recently in the success of television programming such as *The Walking Dead, Riverdale,* and *Teen Wolf,* where teens confront the possibility of their own mortality. Videogames such as *The Legend of Zelda* provide an opportunity to engage in "hack and slash" style combat with a host of weapons from bombs and magic swords to killer boomerangs while dying and being revived by fairies in their efforts to rescue Princess Zelda. With the suicide rates for adolescent boys and girls having been steadily rising since 2000 (Miron et al., 2019), the task of learning to differentiate between the real and the imaginary audience is especially critical.

Counselor educator Ann Vernon (2002) presents the case of 17-year-old Stacie, who contacted her school counselor to discuss her relationship with her boyfriend. According to Stacie, the relationship had been very good for the first few months, but lately they had been arguing so much that she was afraid Matt would break up with her. Whenever they went out, she constantly wanted reassurance that he cared about her, which irritated him. When she persisted, he ignored her. If he didn't call when he said he would, she got anxious and was upset if he didn't return her phone calls right away. She was certain he was seeing other girls and assumed that there was something wrong with her. Her response to this situation was to sit home and wait for his phone calls, call his friends to see where he was, and stay awake at night thinking about the situation. She felt depressed and anxious.

In talking with Stacie further, it appeared that the majority of arguments occurred because Stacie wanted to spend all her time with Matt, and he insisted on having some space. Stacie expressed concern about what he would do if he wasn't with her, so the counselor had her make a list of all the things that could happen. In the next column, she asked Stacie to put a check next to the things that she could prove had happened. Once this was completed, the counselor explained that there was a difference between probability and possibility and that one way of distinguishing between these was to look at past evidence. For example, it was possible that Matt could take out another girl, but to her knowledge had he ever done this? It was possible that he could get killed in a car accident, but had he ever driven recklessly or while drunk when she had been with him? The counselor instructed Stacie to use this type of questioning to deal with her anxiety about things that could happen but seemed unlikely based on history and information about Matt. When Stacie left the session, she admitted feeling less anxious and indicated she had several things she could work on to help her deal with this relationship issue. (p. 335)

In working with Stacie, the counselor first identified the source of her anxiety as stemming from her anticipation that Matt would leave her. Assuming there must be something wrong with her, she became depressed in the face of her loss of self-esteem. In helping her to think through the evidence to support these conclusions, the counselor helped her imagine a more realistic future relationship and practice new behaviors to use in managing her relationship going forward.

The notion of an imaginary audience helps to explain much of the adolescent's reactions to loss. Research suggests the necessity of a broader model for the explanation of adolescent egocentrism, however. Today, researchers favor an integrated account to explain broad changes in adolescent thinking that is achieved principally through the assembly of an advanced "executive suite" of capabilities. These capabilities are influenced by pubertal, cognitive, social, emotional, and psychodynamic factors (Lapsley, 1993) that defy any simple explanation for how adolescents think.

More than anything else, adolescence has been described as a stage transition from childhood to adulthood (*Journal of Adolescence*, 2018; Lerner & Steinberg, 2009). Critics have criticized the concept as an "invention" of modern culture (Fasik, 1994), however, that is an "unnecessary period of life"

(Epstein, 2010). Nonetheless, the longstanding claim by Demos and Demos (1969) that "the idea of adolescence is today one of our most widely held and deeply imbedded assumptions about the process of human development" (p. 632) continues to be supported by a robust body of transdisciplinary, cross-cultural research calling for an expanded and integrated definition (Hewlett, 2013).

It may be more than a simple metaphor to think of the adolescent's transition to adult status as the death of his or her identity as a child. Consistent with our constructivist framework, the journey from childhood through adolescence might be characterized as a developmental process that demands successively more complex solutions to the problems of separation anxiety. From birth through weaning through toilet-training through going to school to leaving home, the child's growth toward adulthood involves increasing separation from caregivers. For the adolescent, this transformation takes the form of a separation of self from society in efforts to integrate into it. The drive toward adulthood requires emancipation from the parents and from the self of childhood. Adolescence can end only when childhood identifications have been subordinated to new identifications. The assumption of adult roles and responsibilities requires that the adolescent abandon the playful aspects of childhood that prevent such an integration.

Although the process is slow and unlikely to be firmly resolved even during high school, the inevitability of graduation forces the reality of a transition upon the adolescent. It has been my experience with high school students completing their coursework in the spring of their senior year that they were not only finishing my course, but were also finishing the day, week, semester, school year, and their public school experience all at the same time. In short, graduation means saying goodbye to childhood. For high school seniors, graduation represents a threat to their individual and collective existence. It is not stretching the comparison too much to note the tradition attached to a graduation ceremony—the gathering of distant relatives, the black graduation robes, a benediction, the speeches by those who knew the "departing" well, and the reading of the "class will." Unlike any other funeral, in the case of our high school seniors, the dead person and the survivor are one and the same. In the senior year of high school, we have what can be viewed as a state of *anticipatory grief.* Faced with the impending reality that "the end is near," the adolescent is torn by a struggle between a secure past in childhood and a seemingly indeterminate future beyond high school. However incomplete the conception may be, adulthood represents a world of hazardous and complex problems for the adolescent.

LOSS AND DISSOLUTION

If adolescence is a period of identity formation, death is not so much the end of life as it is the end of existence. Death can bring a new existence in the minds of adolescents unless, of course, no one cares, and they are forgotten. Like the wicked witch in the Land of Oz, true death comes with the end of "my beautiful wickedness [as] I am melting, melting. . . . " Loss for the adolescent comes with the dissolution of one's boundaries, the loss of purpose or meaning for one's existence, and the failure of reality to live up to one's own expectations. Friendships are created and destroyed as spontaneously as anticipation collides with reality. Roles are re-examined and the gods, who were our parents, become traitors, then failures, and finally just people.

This theme is captured beautifully in Arthur Miller's (1976/1949) *Death of a Salesman* as the play traces the decay of a god—Willy Loman, Salesman-Lord of New England. The illusion of sexless godhood is destroyed when the 17-year-old Biff finds Willy with a strange woman. The tragedy lies in Biff's failure to accept his father as a sexual person and in his failure to profit from his father's example. Instead, Biff rejects his father's pleas for forgiveness and leaves home for a "couple of babes," much as his father had done before him.

More than with any other group, adolescents are influenced by the context in which their communications occur. Aware of their own thoughts and feelings about loss, adolescents need opportunities to experience their losses and share their personal reactions in public. Reflecting on their egocentrism, adolescents are likely to believe that others are aware of how they feel, but that others can't possibly understand their unique, personal experience (Lapsley, 1993). Elkind (1974) speculates that the adolescent's

> belief in a personal uniqueness becomes a conviction that he will not die, that death will happen to others but not to him. This complex of beliefs in the uniqueness of his feelings and of his immortality might be called *a personal fable,* a story which he tells himself and which is not true. (p. 93)

As participant observers in their own life dramas, adolescents are now witness to their own unmet expectations. Springer and Wallerstein (1983) noted in their work with divorced families that young adolescents "grieved not only the loss of their intact families, but also, the loss of the kind of intact family they had never had and now would never attain" (p. 18). The personal fable associated with the perfect family one would have had, if only this or that hadn't happened, can present a formidable obstacle in the adolescent's successful resolution of the loss associated with divorce.

MEDIATING IN LOSS

The challenge for those who care for adolescents is to help them make better choices in facing life directly. If caregivers are to help adolescents understand the losses they experience, they must understand the adolescent's efforts to make meaning of the events. To be effective in helping adolescents cope with loss, caregivers must understand how adolescents make sense of loss. If change and loss are inevitable, and if the experience associated with loss is related to one's capacity to make sense of that change, young people need to know about changes that can affect their lives. This work involves helping them to acknowledge the loss rather than fight it and necessitates increasing the range of possible responses to change.

Adolescents require adult guides who will encourage them to express their feelings and help them understand their pain as a reaction to the loss they experience. Once the feelings associated with the loss have been acknowledged, caregivers should seek to mediate in that space between the loss and the adolescent's experience of that loss. It is in this gap that the adolescent must make sense of the self that is no longer me and the new self that is yet to come. Caregivers must listen to the adolescent's questions and ask themselves what these questions tell them about the adolescent's efforts to make sense of what has happened. Understanding the hows and whys of the events that lead to any loss can give meaning to the chaotic feelings that accompany loss and help guide future behavior in addressing similar losses.

Because developmental tasks are mastered sequentially, familiarity with the individual's developmental tempo can help identify when an individual lags behind his or her own developmental pace. When working with adolescents, caregivers are often confronted with helping them to make sense of a loss that happened some time ago. As noted in working with children, the ongoing process of grief means that prior experience with loss will need to be re-examined yet again. It's particularly difficult to help adolescents through losses that reflect perceived lapses in judgment, such as abuse, abandonment, mental illness, imprisonment, substance abuse, or suicide. In such cases, caregivers should ask themselves what similar needs or experiences the adolescent might have had. Is there anything that might be misunderstood or for which the adolescent might feel responsible? And critically, is there any action by the parent that the child might feel compelled to repeat?

As the adolescent is becoming aware, parents and other "grown-ups" are not as they have seemed. The adolescent's successful transition to adulthood involves a redefinition of what it is to be an adult—the projection of a new self into which to grow. Growth begins with separating from the past culture of childhood and the adolescent's outmoded perspective on adulthood.

Rightfully, parents feel rejected, but it is not they, but rather their child's former understanding of them that is being rejected. In the adolescent's quest for greater autonomy, the desire for privacy complicates the need for adult monitoring. Critically, the availability of a caring and responsive adult has been shown to be the best predictor of positive outcomes for grieving adolescents (Worden, 2018). While the adolescent is busy building a new set of parents, therefore, it is vitally important that the parents hold still, providing a stable and thereby reliable point of reference.

> Many a parent new to living with an adolescent has come to me seeking advice on how best to live with this "stranger" in their house. They explain that they have tried everything "to get through to" their child, without any appreciable results. Indeed, things often appear worse despite their efforts to accommodate the often unreasonable demands of these quasi-adults. "What else am I to do?" they ask. "Nothing," I reply, and then add quickly: "But, let me explain. Consider a lighthouse, perched close by the edge of the sea at the most dangerous precipice along the coast. Now consider the ship at sea, floundering about in the dark, guided only by a light in the distance that signals: 'Danger, keep away.' How can it possibly help? Ironically, the lighthouse shows the wary sailor where not to go, and in so doing, steers the wise captain away from certain danger."
>
> "Consider instead, what it would be like navigating in the dark if the keeper of the lighthouse were to take down the light and set out with it in another boat to meet the ship at sea. With each effort by the keeper to approach the ship, its captain would turn away instead. Guided by the movements of the ship, however, the keeper would persist in the chase, moving about in uncertain circles. Although not inevitable, the possibilities for disaster are greatly enhanced as both the lighthouse keeper and the sailor depend solely upon the sailor's attempts to make safe passage."

So too, the adolescent is guided by a figure in the dark, a parent who stands by but also for something of great significance. Absorbed in their own newfound sense of importance, adolescents misunderstand the danger inherent in steering a course for their parents. They overestimate their abilities to sail their own course. Nonetheless, the resolute parent is a far better guide than the one who sets sail on the seas of adolescence to negotiate a course that is undetermined.

Such is the plight of the parent who attempts to "befriend" rather than "parent" an adolescent. By holding still, adults help adolescents to recover from the losses of childhood. In separating from their parents, adolescents can find them anew. From the adolescent's perspective, however, we have a very different understanding of the situation. Recalling the constructivist's notion that reality is invented, not discovered, Watzlawick (1984) proffers a useful extension of our metaphor:

A captain who on a dark, stormy night has to sail through an uncharted channel, devoid of beacons and other navigational aids, will either wreck his ship on the cliffs or regain the safe, open sea beyond the strait. If he loses ship and life, his failure proves that the course he steered was not the right one. One may say that he discovered what the passage was not. If, on the other hand, he clears the strait, this success merely proves that he literally did not at any point come into collision with the (otherwise unknown) shape and nature of the waterway; it tells him nothing about how safe or how close to disaster he was at any given moment. (pp. 14–15)

It's important to note that our adolescent captain has set a rather ambiguous course to navigate the channel without parental guidance or other "navigational aids." Further, we haven't taken account of fellow passengers on this voyage, (i.e., peers and other well-meaning adults along for the ride and offering their own conjecture on the best path to open seas). And finally, the "success or failure" of the voyage is a life journey under construction, where each change during the journey inevitably leads to yet other changes that challenge the adolescent once more.

Critically, our adolescent captain has only been aware of what doesn't work, informed by the failure of prior assumptions about the best course forward. The "best course" is a matter of historical interpretation, however, based on the *viability* not the *correctness* of the chosen path. In a particular irony, it is only through loss that these assumptive realities reveal themselves. In effect, we only become fully aware of the meaning we have made in our lives through reflecting upon the losses we recognize and through the process of meaning reconstruction that leads to a new reality.

In helping the adolescent through this process, the first thing to communicate is that "You are not alone; I am with you" as a balance to magical and egocentric thinking. Accurate information and an adult perspective on the facts of the loss should be provided as directly as possible to relieve blame and re-establish accurate self-perceptions. When talking about loss, the focus should be on the adolescent's experience. This focus helps them to reveal their own understanding of the associated events and gives them permission to trust their own judgments about the situation while making it harder to deny the loss in the future. When approaching an impending change, adolescents should be told how their routines and lifestyles will be affected to increase their sense of control over their own lives. By helping adolescents master the facts of their existence, caregivers can help them expand their vocabulary of feelings and thoughts about loss and its resolution.

Particularly important in working with adolescents is to acknowledge the profound effect the imaginary audience of one's peers is likely to have in any interpretation of loss and its resolution. Anxious about the reactions of one's peers, adolescents may reach out to the Internet for comfort and support only to experience "increased fears around predictability, increased social dismissal, and elevated self-doubt" (Wheat & Whiting, 2018, p. 98). Complicating matters for the grieving adolescent is the possibility of being dismissed as wearisome by friends. In complementary fashion, the friends are likely to struggle with their own loss of a stable and reliable relationship with the now grieving friend. In working with adolescents, therefore, one should place them in groups with peers who may be experiencing similar losses. As the imaginary audience is progressively modified to conform to the reactions of the real audience, the adolescent can begin to form relationships that are more mutual than self-interested. Losses can be evaluated more objectively and one's reactions shared interpersonally with others whose feelings are gradually integrated with one's own. As with younger children, bibliotherapy offers the adolescent an opportunity to identify with others and, in confronting the personal fable of their experience as unique, can help them to realize they are not alone.

A BRIDGE TOO FAR

Somewhere between the struggles for identity that act themselves out in adolescence and the stability that comes with finding oneself at peace with society, there exists a stage social psychologist Kenneth Keniston (1970) calls *youth.* The newly evolved self of adolescence now exists in a dynamic tension with the society in which it was once embedded. Keniston explained that "the adolescent is struggling to define who he is; the youth begins to sense who he is and thus to recognize the possibility of conflict and disparity between his emerging selfhood and his social order" (p. 636). Confident of the identity newly constructed in adolescence, youth have yet to develop an understanding of the larger social world sufficient to support their nascent efforts to live *as* rather than just *with* adults. For youth, the journey from adolescence to adulthood is yet a bridge too far.

In youth there exists a "pervasive ambivalence" (Keniston, 1970) toward both self and society. This ambivalence is acted out in conflicts between maintaining an autonomous self and being committed in some social involvement. The fear is that the newly developed self will be lost in a world not yet fully understood. The irony comes with the recognition that in failing to make commitments, the self is lost in not being all that it can be. Development is valued for itself, change is actively sought, and motion, in all its forms, becomes the goal. In youth, as in all other stages of life, *the fear of death* takes a special form:

For the infant, to be deprived of maternal support, responsiveness, and care is not to exist. For the 4-year-old, nonbeing means loss of body intactness (e.g., dismemberment, mutilation, castration). For the adolescent, to cease to be is to fall apart, to fragment, splinter, or diffuse into nothingness. For the youth, however, to lose one's essential vitality is merely to stop. . . . To "grow up" is in some ultimate sense to cease to really be alive. (Keniston, 1970, p. 640)

Building on the pioneering work of Erikson (1968), Keniston (1970), Levinson (1978), and Perry (1970), psychologist Jeffrey Arnett (2000) proposed the term *emerging adulthood* to describe this period from ages 18 to 24 as distinct from adolescence and young adulthood. As defined, emerging adulthood "is a period characterized by change and exploration for most people, as they examine the life possibilities open to them and gradually arrive at more enduring choices in love, work, and worldviews" (Arnett, 2000, p. 480).

Youth are ambivalent about their status as adults. No longer adolescents, they nonetheless have difficulty seeing themselves as adults. Typically, they have yet to attain the traditional markers of adulthood such as home ownership, finishing school, settling into a career, and being committed to a long-term love relationship. Surprisingly, these demographic transitions rank among the least important concerns for youth. Instead, their top criteria for transition to adulthood are accepting responsibility for one's self, making independent decisions, and becoming financially independent (Arnett et al., 2011; Nelson & Barry, 2005). The losses of youth are characterized by the "great expectations" that so often go unmet. Earlier failures to separate are echoed in the youth's reluctance to adapt to the new experiences of leaving home for college, work, marriage, or travel. As Arnett (2000) has poignantly observed:

Explorations in love sometimes result in disappointment, disillusionment, or rejection. Explorations in work sometimes result in failure to find work that is satisfying and fulfilling. Explorations in worldviews sometimes lead to rejection of childhood beliefs without the construction of anything more compelling in their place. (p. 473)

Recognizing youth as a period of experimentation and exploration, Nelson and Barry (2005) acknowledge that it is also a time of instability and uncertainty for some people. In support, they cite the separation, loneliness, exploration, and failure that youth face as lending themselves to the possibility of depression. Although researchers have concluded that anyone can feel lonely at any time (Cacioppo et al., 2015), the ambivalence that comes from wanting to find oneself through some commitment and the fear of losing oneself in the process make young people the loneliest people in America (Perlman, 1990; Qualter et al., 2015).

The central struggle of personality to achieve an appropriate balance between attachment and individuation, between dependence and independence, between self-absorption and a commitment to others, is acted out again on a new plane in youth. Critically, researchers found that American youth who had the most frequent contact with their parents, especially those still living at home, tended to have the poorest relationships with their parents and the poorest psychological adjustment (O'Connor et al., 1996).

The task that lies before youth is to separate not only self from parents, but also self from parents as a source of judgments and expectations about the self. Working within this context, caregivers must help youth to clarify the basis of their own judgments without simultaneously giving in to the temptation to replace the parents as a source of new judgments and new expectations. In a quote commonly attributed to Mark Twain, a youth's newly revised judgment of his father is poignantly, if not comically, on display:

> When I was a boy of fourteen, my father was so ignorant I could hardly stand to have the old man around. But when I got to be twenty-one, I was astonished at how much he had learned in seven years." (Quote Investigator, 2010)

The goal is to help youth to accept themselves as "parents"—to accept the challenge to entertain the possibility of change and be in charge of themselves. In meeting this challenge, youth need to realize that many of the changes they experience and thus the losses they encounter are of their own making. Having thrown over parents as a source of judgment and without having come to some understanding of their own self-efficacy, youth often lose their motivation. The shift in the balance of self and others' expectations of self raises the question of who is in charge. The challenge for youth is how to integrate a view of themselves as independent agents (something for which they have strived so long) with the understanding that they are dependent upon others (something from which they have been trying to emerge). This dilemma of youth is resolved when autonomy takes the form of self-commitment to some social activity.

Traditionally, political activism, religious conversion, Greek life, or a company-sponsored group activity have prepared the way to marriage as the most popular social vehicle for this resolution. Today's youth appear to have been forced to reconsider this path to adulthood. Faced with a steady erosion of the assumptive realities of home ownership, financial independence, being capable of managing a household, raising children, and being personally responsible, youth have become ambivalent about making adult commitments. Due to a combination of economic and social factors such as rising housing costs, heavy college debt, underemployment, and increased employment opportunities for women outside the home, the proportion of adults aged 25–34 who continue to live with their parents nearly doubled between 2000 and 2017 (Choi et al., 2019). This ambivalence about making adult commitments is seen as well in the steady climb in the average age for first marriage (U.S. Census Bureau, 2019). As well, witness the current use of the term "snowflake" to refer to youth who appear too convinced of their own uniqueness to be able (or bothered) to handle what they consider to be the harsh realities of the world. Having thrown over parents as a source of judgment, today's youth appear yet to come to some understanding of their own self-efficacy. Without having found a balance between self and others' expectations, they appear to have opted to leave no one in charge.

Failure to find this balance places lasting constraints on the ability to form deep and committed relationships in adult life. As Erikson (1968) cautioned. "It is only when identity formation is well on its way that true intimacy—which is really a counterpointing as well as fusing of identities—is possible" (p. 135). Developing the capacity for true intimacy is a long process that will require extensive life experience coupled with considerable self-reflection.

MEDIATING IN LOSS

In working with youth, adults are cautioned to avoid cooperating in the paradox their behavior presents. Given acknowledgment of their adult status, youth often behave like children. In earlier developmental periods, giving up the self in the face of change was done with great reluctance. The myths that resolving loss is painful, or that it takes a long time, or that giving up the outworn means losing something important, are replaced with a new myth that change in and of itself is good. For youth, who seek change as an antidote to death, a headlong leap into experimentation seems in order. It should come as no surprise that high risk behaviors such as unprotected sex, binge drinking, and driving at high speeds reach their peak during youth (Arnett, 2000).

Youth are only *provisional adults,* who require opportunities to exercise their newfound selves *in* society. Engagement in political activism can provide a bridging environment for youth that acknowledges their efforts to make autonomous decisions without either promoting anarchy or abandoning them to fend for themselves. Yet, they also need clear signals about the consequences of their actions for others. College students, for example, should be helped to see that failure can be positive feedback to faculty members who see advisement as little more than hand holding. To be able to enter into youths' efforts to make meaning of their independence without making that meaning for them is a great challenge to one's own independence. Moreover, ideas that conflict with one's prior experience needn't represent an existential threat to one's continued existence.

Caregivers must help youth to clarify the basis of their own judgments without simultaneously giving in to the temptation to replace the parents as a source of new judgments and new expectations. The goal is to help youth to accept themselves as "parents"—to accept the possibility for change and be in charge of themselves. Adults can play a critical role in fostering this development by providing real-life examples of persons who have made choices and are living with the consequences. By breaking down complex tasks into manageable steps, caregivers can model appropriate behaviors. Serving as mentors, they can help youth to understand their current social context more fully, envision a more desirable future, and help guide them on a path to realizing that future. Critically, caregivers should encourage youth to work through the process by making their own choices, examining the outcomes, and living with the consequences.

In sum, youth are served best by active engagement in a caring community that is intellectually challenging, emotionally supportive, and provides the structure and breadth of experience necessary to build a strong sense of self in relationship with people and social institutions. As will become apparent in the chapters to follow, the self one has constructed in youth provides the platform from which future selves are launched in adulthood. The richer the set of experiences that helped shape us as youth, the more resilient and adaptable we are likely to be in transcending the losses that lie ahead.

NOTE

Adapted from R. L. Hayes. (1981). High school graduation: The case for identity loss. *Personnel and Guidance Journal, 59*, 369–371. Republished with permission of the American Counseling Association conveyed through Copyright Clearance Center, Inc.; R. L. Hayes. (1986). Human growth and development. In M. Lewis, R. L. Hayes, & J. Lewis (Eds.), *An introduction to the counseling profession* (pp. 36–95). Itasca, IL: F. E. Peacock. Republished with permission of the author; Hayes, R. L. (2020). *Making meaning: A constructivist approach to counseling and groupwork in education*. Washington, DC: Lexington/Rowman & Littlefield. Republished with permission of Lexington/Rowman & Littlefield.

Chapter 7

Midlife

Adulthood is marked by a constellation of major losses: changes in parental role due to children leaving home for college or work; the onset of more frequent and disabling physical conditions; diminished procreative and sexual functioning; changes in physical appearance due to the relentless force of gravity; recognition that one may have plateaued professionally; the recurring sense that time remaining to accomplish all one dreamed is shrinking; and the death of older relatives and family friends. Of course, with loss comes opportunity. But opportunity brings other changes that bring other losses and new challenges. A new job, even if a better one, may mean changes in residence, lifestyle, friends or colleagues, work responsibilities, work habits, social obligations, how one is regarded by others, and demands on one's time and energies, all of which contribute to potential changes in the relationship between oneself and a partner or other family members.

And yet, changes in family constellation can provide opportunities to try new roles and engage in new activities. Physical limitations may encourage new forms of exercise or changes in diet. Changing physical appearance may occasion surgical or cosmetic remedies or promote a reappraisal of one's concept of beauty. Changes in sexual activity may lead to a reappraisal of one's notions of intimacy. And long-delayed plans may be accelerated, modified, or abandoned altogether. As writer Kathryn Schulz (2022) observed:

> We are almost always facing more than one thing at once and therefore feeling more than one thing at once. We feel sympathy together with self-pity, good fortune together with frustration, gratitude together with grief. . . . All these are examples of what I think of as the fundamental *and*-ness of life, the way it requires us to experience so many contradictory or unrelated things all at once. There's no getting away from this *and*-ness *because* it is built into the basic facts of our existence. (para. 7–10 [emphases in original])

This sense of "and-ness" in life is the essential experience of living in that space between life as we have known it and the possibility of a life to be realized. It is in this space that meaning is made, where loss meets opportunity and the challenge to face life anew presents itself. Whether we embrace or resist the change that brought us to this point, loss will demand we make meaning of the experience.

There is a rich literature on managing grief and loss (e.g., Amazon books listed more than 40,000 titles in the first 90 days of 2022 with 78 more "coming soon"). Instead, the concern here is not so much with what we do in response to any loss as it is with the experience of loss that change initiates. Because our notions of "reality" undergo constant revision, loss is experienced in the moment of the event within our meaning-making systems. Unlike the relatively naive systems employed by children, adolescents and youth, the meanings made by adults have been built over decades of experiences with loss and organized into a complex constellation of assumptions. This *assumptive world* (Kauffman, 2002) reflects all that we believe to be true about ourselves and the world. It gives a sense of purpose and meaning that guides our expectations. These assumptions about the purpose of life, the nature of justice, or one's self-worth, for example, are revealed in the stories we tell, especially about ourselves.

Geoff was a 47-year-old single male who came to me to find more effective ways to enhance his relationship with his ailing mother. He had just moved "back home" to assist her in recovering from surgery following a fall. Although he reported that their relationship had "never been exactly ideal," he believed that it might be improved if only he could find a way to please her. "But," he offered, "no matter what I do, she's never happy."

In an attempt to ground his expectations for the "ideal," I asked, "What would it look like if she were happy?" "I . . . I don't really know," came the hesitant reply. "I guess I'd like her to just once thank me for what I've done for her instead of telling me how it could have been better or different or more or whatever. It just seems that no matter what I do, I can never make my mother happy." The discussion turned rather quickly to the telling of a litany of past efforts that failed to please his mother and, in due course, to the introduction of his younger brother who it seemed "could do no wrong." "No matter what I do, I can NEVER make her happy," he concluded, putting the stress on "never."

"And yet you continue to try," I said, noting the irony in his conclusion. "Yes, I suppose I do," he admitted reluctantly. "It's just that my brother doesn't even try to make her happy and here I am trying all the time. And it never works for me. It just doesn't seem fair," he protested. "I just can't make her happy."

"I hear what you're saying but I'm not sure you've entirely listened to yourself," I offered. "Let me ask you to repeat yourself: 'No matter what I do, I can never make my mother happy.'"

"Yes, that's it exactly. That's my whole point. I can NEVER make her happy," he reasserted, again stressing that this was never going to happen despite his persistent efforts to try. I then asked him to try the sentence again, but this time putting the stress on "I" rather than on "never." After a few false starts reverting to putting the emphasis on "never," he hesitantly repeated, as if hearing these words for the first time, stressing "I" rather than "never," "No matter what I do, I can never make my mother happy." And then, as if lightning had struck his chair, he bolted upright and shouted, "No matter what I do, I can never make my mother happy." He said it again and again each time louder, each time with greater conviction, and each time with the emphasis on his own lack of agency as if he were speaking a great truth that had somehow eluded him until now. There is nothing HE could do to make her happy.

We talked for a while longer about his insight, about what this said about the person he has been, and what he might have to give up. We explored what it would mean for his behavior going forward, and how he might relate differently to his mother knowing that he would never be her "favorite." And what would it mean if he accepted that there was nothing he could do to make her happy? We spoke of his growing sense of how much he had lost in trying to please his mother over the years and how small that had made him feel. As we wrapped up, he reflected: "I just feel so free, as if a great weight has been lifted. I understand now that her rejection isn't my fault. I'm still a good person even if she doesn't appreciate all I do. For now, I think that might be enough."

THE STORIES WE TELL

As argued, people make meaning of their present concerns within the context of their own construction of the past. From this perspective, we serve as our own historians. In confronting the past, we must consider whether to treat it as menacing and unknown or as a way to organize our thoughts and feelings for assimilation. The meaning we make of any change will be informed by the varying degrees of congruence and incongruence with our current beliefs and expectations about what we have to lose. The extent to which each experience reinforces or discourages our current understanding will shape the self-narrative we take into future encounters.

A narrative is not just an ordinary re-telling of a data set. It is a story with a perspective. It is intended to make a point. As Rappaport (2000) explains: "We seem to experience our lives as storied in part because that helps us see the point, *to see meaning in our lives*" (p. 4; emphasis added). Who we are and who we are becoming are intimately intertwined with the meanings we make of our experience, especially related to loss. The chief means toward this end, however, is the reenactment of the past in our own minds. Whether we cast ourselves as heroes or victims, saviors or saints, winners or losers, we are the authors of the stories we tell. As Rodgers and Scott (2008) argue, there is a "notion of continuity and coherence that signals a self, even as there are discontinuities, shifts, and crises that signal an *evolving* [emphasis in original] self. In effect, the self can be seen as *the meaning-maker, or teller of stories* [emphasis added]" (p. 738). Because the sets of events used to compose a life are experienced uniquely, each person's life is its own grand narrative.

In reconstructing the past, the process taking place in the person's mind reflects present understanding set in the current social context. As previously constructed, former reality is not necessarily congruent with present understanding. Thus, personal narratives may be seen more as fabrication than as re-creation (Brown & Augusta-Scott, 2007; Chiari & Nuzzo, 2010; Freeman, 2015). In storytelling, it is the ordering of events (whether real or fictional) in time that reveals the mind of the teller, not the facts per se. To understand narrative is to appreciate what one holds to be true. It's not so much that people *have* problems as much as they *experience* problems. Thus, a person whose stories define "a phenomenon as a 'problem' will be stuck with attempted solutions that are logically consistent with those stories" (Becvar et al., 1997, p. 21) unless and until they re-story that phenomenon in favor of a more viable narrative.

Ruth and I met over dinner at the home of a mutual friend. She introduced herself as a management consultant and related that she had occasion to travel frequently as part of her work. "That must be interesting work," I ventured.

"The work, yes," she replied, "but the travel is hell. All that waiting in line at airports, jammed into a van to get to today's hotel, only to be dumped into a crowded lobby, more waiting in line at the registration desk, and then the ride in an elevator to search endless corridors for my room and a safe place to rest at last."

"It all sounds a bit overwhelming. How do you manage?" I wondered aloud. In response, she took me through a set of alternative strategies she had developed over the years to avoid the crushing anxiety that these encounters created: a membership in the airport travel club to provide a refuge from the crowded terminal, driving herself to the airport to avoid using a shuttle bus, taking early and late flights that are typically less crowded, getting first floor rooms near the lobby to avoid the elevator and the search down corridors, and "I guess I've just accepted that I'm not a very brave person and just deal with it as best I can," she concluded.

Over the course of the evening, we had the chance to talk more. I was impressed with her courage and her determination. Equally impressive was her creativity in starting her own business and in meeting the challenges of travel. Her concern for the family that she often "left behind" was balanced by her gratitude for their continued support and faith in her. The emerging picture seemed at odds with how she had described herself. I learned as well that she had grown up in a Jewish home where she shared a bed as a young girl with her beloved grandmother Nannie. Each evening as they prepared for sleep, Nannie would tell her stories of being sent to America as a young girl to avoid the rising anti-Semitism in her native Austria. She learned of the state-sponsored extermination of the Jews by the Nazis, of the families jammed into railroad cars for transport to crowded death camps only to stand in line awaiting reassignment to work or one's death. She learned of the heroism of those Jews who resisted, of the courage of those who remained resolute in their faith even in the face of death, and of her Nannie's gratitude to her parents for saving her life while all who remained died in Auschwitz. Nannie's was a cautionary tale not to trust too much and to hold fast to one's family. Ruth, it seemed, found herself trusting too little and feared losing her family as well.

Having been introduced as a psychologist, I was asked if you could "catch a story." "Like the flu or a cold?" I asked. "Yes, I think people do hear stories that can have a profound effect on how they see the world and how they behave. As I've listened to you tell the story of your Nannie, I've been struck how similar that is to the story you tell of your work: the crowds, the enclosed spaces, the helplessness, the anxiety, the inevitable separation from your family. But I also hear the courage, the determination, and the gratitude. I wonder, do you think they're related?"

As is often the case at such gatherings, other guests and conversations interrupted ours, and we were left without an answer to my question. Weeks later we had a chance to meet once again and spoke for only a few minutes. "I want to thank you," she began. "I've been thinking about your question, about how my story is maybe my Nannie's as well. And yes, I think so. And I've been thinking about how it ends, how it could end differently. I've come to appreciate it's not just a story about loss but about having the courage to go on, the determination to do what's right, and to be grateful for who you are and what you have."

Putting on my counselor's hat, I asked, "How's that going for you?" And as quickly as the smile that came to her face, she declared, "I still don't like travelling much but I've come to see it as a privilege. So, I treat my anxiety as a reminder of my good fortune and how grateful I am for all who've made my life possible."

Narrative reconstruction challenges existing constructions of how we understand ourselves, others, and our life course. In restorying her work life, Ruth was able to confront the assumption that she lived in a hostile world where she had to protect herself from anticipated losses. Instead, she transformed her view of herself as a potential victim into a woman who was grateful for the support of a family that appreciated her sacrifice on their behalf. In this way,

> restorying experience becomes a central component of healing [where] creating new meaning structures causes experience to be considered from another perspective, reorganizes the elements of old story lines, creates new symbolic structures for comprehending living, and promotes mastery over experiences that were formerly unmanageable. (Hansen, 2006, p. 293)

INTENDING AN AUDIENCE

In understanding the meanings people give to these stories, it's important to account for the purpose and the social context of these narratives. As Pride (2002) argues: "Stories make meaning of life. The stories we tell each other, and particularly the stories we insist others learn, not only contain knowledge of our selves and our past but they intend a distinct future" (pp. 1–2). The stories we tell are intended to connect events in a meaningful way for a definite audience. They are meant to provide insight into that world as a guide to future behavior.

> Some thirty-five years ago, I was engaged in a casual conversation with a university colleague who remarked: "I grew up hating Catholics, but I have no idea why." As the conversation continued, we explored the myriad ways in which early experience, media, and the teachings of respected elders had shaped this prejudice. In the end we were comforted by the self-affirming (if not self-deceptive) belief that we both had transcended such assumptions about religion as well as race and gender. Yet, the question remained for me: how do we learn to hate? And, having understood its origins, how do we transcend such ideas in ourselves and resist perpetuating those prejudices in the generations to follow?

Any effort to understand what maintains cultural stereotypes necessarily involves the identification, construction, deconstruction, and reconstruction of social narratives. Complicating this calculation is the reality that there are things that we "know" of which we are unaware. These assumptive realities were formed long ago and have withstood disconfirmation. They have become so "normalized" that they remain persistently out of awareness. By way of example, we can understand the origins of my colleague's "unexamined" hatred of Catholics by knowing that he grew up in South Carolina in a community populated by descendants of French Huguenots. Their forebears had settled there more than 300 years earlier to escape religious persecution at the hands of successive Catholic kings. The story of their persecution and "le refuge" provided the dominant narrative to fuel his prejudice. Embedded in what I call "the ambient conversation" of daily life, my colleague came to adopt, if not fully understand, the centuries-old notion that one should be wary of Catholics.

So too, many of the habits related to food, personal hygiene, and social customs that we carry into adult life have their origins in the magical thinking of childhood and the reinforcing capacity of culture to shape the narratives we claim as our own.

To this day, 45 years of marriage hasn't changed that I find myself powerless to leave anything on my plate as evidence that I appreciate the sacrifice made by the host and Mother Nature in providing this meal for me. Similarly, my wife is compelled to leave some scrap, no matter how small the meal, as testimony that the host had prepared enough. As a compromise, I wait until she's finished and then eat what's left on her plate. In this way, we both preserve the assumptions we've brought from childhood without the necessity to revise our world view of ourselves as "good and responsible" people (at least over dinner).

Our early encounters with loss and our efforts at understanding are shaped by the reactions of those around us. How we learn to cope with loss in all its forms and the set of experiences that frame this journey are acted out in the larger context of the social environment life offers us.

THE DEVELOPING ADULT

A central thesis of this book is that some change in human development is the outcome of all effective counseling and psychotherapy. An understanding of human development helps us make sense of peoples' behaviors in facing the losses that arise from change over the lifespan. Rather than view development as a series of distinct stages, each with its own characteristic challenges and developing capabilities, it may be more appropriate to think of one's life as a "movement through forms" (Basseches, 2005). Over the course of development, people show qualitative differences in how they make meaning of a greater variety of experience. Notably, this process for understanding change and loss does not end with adolescence or youth. The development of our understanding of the world and the meaning we give to our experience of it can continue over a lifetime. Because earlier levels of understanding are nested within more advanced levels, however, adults have the capacity to understand children while the reverse awaits the development of new cognitive capacities.

Humans do not develop in a vacuum, however. We are creatures living in a time and place with other creatures engaged in transactions between ourselves as meaning-makers and our personal surroundings. The life we experience and the meaning we make of loss may be our own subjective construction, but this construction is limited by the environmental framework in which it takes place. Accounting for an individual's efforts to make meaning of loss is complicated by demographic and psychological characteristics, personal experiences, and cultural practices (Harter, 2012; Overton & Muller, 2013; Siegler et al., 2017). Moreover, this activity takes place in a "river" of personal relationships, social, religious, and governmental systems, and cultures that simultaneously organize, direct, and evaluate the individual's responses to any loss (Becvar et al., 1997). As Carlsen (1991) poignantly reminds us:

> Part of the experience of "swimming in one's own river" is facing the many forces outside of oneself: neighborhoods, relationships, culture and history, stereotypes and prejudice, economic conditions, job opportunity, living arrangements. Then, of course, there are all those other matters such as genetics, accidents, and patterns of health and decline in the history of one's family. The fruit that one is handed from the family tree is not always good for one's health. But one has some choices in how one processes that fruit. (p. 24)

Despite where we find ourselves in the river, it is our experience in the moment that shapes our world. If we accept that we created that world, then we have the power to change it. The question remains as to how one learns to swim well.

COMPOSING A LIFE

Taking a lifespan perspective, our lives can be divided into roughly equal thirty-year periods. In this view, middle age extends from roughly sometime in the 30s until sometime in the mid to late 60s, depending upon a whole host of factors, not the least of which are one's health, socio-economic status, and culturally-defined values. Despite this uncertain course, middle age is generally regarded as a "pivotal period in the life course in terms of (a) balancing growth and decline, (b) linking earlier and later periods of life, and (c) bridging younger and older generations" (Lachman et al., 2015, p. 20).

Rather than view midlife as a balance, a link, or a bridge between a life passed and a future life, it is tempting to think of it more as a developmental epoch. As explored in chapter 2, each developmental epoch involves active engagement in adaptation and reorganization of one's intrapersonal and interpersonal worlds, during which basic shifts in thinking, feeling, and behaving must be made. As such, midlife is characterized by intense periods of challenge and discovery, transition and reconciliation, consolidation and growth, reflection and anticipation.

> Recall from chapter 3 that Angel and Andre divorced so that each would not have to change and risk the loss of a carefully constructed identity. As so often happens in divorcing, each partner is forced to make an honest appraisal of who you are and how you want to be with others. In due course, Angel and Andre decided to remain the same and accept the inevitability of their incompatibility. But the changes occasioned by their divorce, prompted further examination by Angel, who sought me out a year into her new status as a divorcee. She

expressed some regret at not having given her marriage to Andre "a second chance," and all she lost in the process. But she took comfort in knowing "he just wasn't gonna change." For her part, meeting other men, comparing experiences with other divorced women, and a bit of reflection on how she could "do things better" had opened her eyes to the possibility of being different somehow. "I think I've still got some wrinkles to iron out," she offered, "but I know I don't want to be that—like I was like with Andre." At the urging of her employer, she had enrolled in a management course at the local community college. There she discovered a world of opportunity beyond her current position and was introduced to a new set of friends. "It's not like it was with Andre. I don't feel like I have to prove I'm right all the time. It just seems they like me like I am."

We met for two more sessions as she explored her changing relationship with others, which she attributed to their willingness to accept her as she is. What she failed to realize was that outside of her relationship with Andre, others felt no need to prove themselves right or her wrong. Instead, they were willing to entertain her views as presented and she, in turn, felt no need to defend herself. In time she came to understand that her "stubbornness" was as much a reaction to the perceived threat that she wasn't "smart enough" as it was about "proving they can't push me around." Buoyed by the social support of new friends, and more confident in her self-appraisal as competent and smart, Angel found herself more comfortable in exploring new relationships and enjoying the possibility of a brighter future for herself.

In an engaging metaphor, Mary Catherine Bateson (1989) offers that one composes a life, much like playing jazz, by combining "familiar and unfamiliar components in response to new situations, following an underlying grammar and an evolving aesthetic" (p. 3). As she explains:

> Today, the materials and skills from which a life is composed are no longer clear. It is no longer possible to follow the paths of previous generations. . . . Our lives not only take new directions; they are subject to repeated redirection, partly because of the extension of our years of health and productivity. Just as the design of a building or of a vase must be rethought when the scale is changed, so must the design of lives. Many of the most basic concepts we use to construct a sense of self, or the design of a life have changed their meanings. Work. Home. Love. Commitment. (Bateson, 1989, p. 2)

All of this is to say that development during midlife is extraordinarily complex. As stated repeatedly, the inevitability of change brings loss to the mind of the person who can appreciate that things are somehow different. Determining what is different, however, is central to and initiates the meaning-making process. As we have seen in Sharon's case (see chapter 2), interpretation of the loss event will change as individual circumstances and the level of meaning-making shift over time. Nonetheless, research supports the conclusion that barely half of adults have attained higher level thinking skills. Moreover, those who demonstrate that they have full formal operational skills don't always use them.

Living in today's multicultural, technologically-sophisticated, and rapidly changing society requires the cognitive capacity to manage ambiguity and to make sense of problems that defy clear or simple answers (Drago-Severson, 2016). The demands of living in a world where problems lack clear definition and resist workable solutions "necessitates an increased complexity of consciousness, and an ability to construct one's own internal belief system, standard, or personal filter that enables one to make meaning of oneself and one's work in new ways" (Helsing et al., 2008, p. 439). These abilities require what adult development theorists call "self-authorship," which is the internal capacity to generate one's own views on the world, oneself, and relationships with others (Baxter Magolda, 2001; Kegan, 2000).

Researchers have found that individuals who operate at these levels of development are seen as being more effective (Strang & Kuhnert, 2009), more strategic (Merron et al., 1987), more collaborative (Bushe & Gibbs, 1990), more critically self-reflective (Mezirow, 2000), and more socially mature and creative (Vaillant & McCullough, 1987). As desirable as these characteristics may be for a person facing the challenges of midlife today, as much as two-thirds of the adult population of the United States has yet to develop these self-authoring capacities (Kegan, 1994). Nonetheless, research supports the possibility of continued advances in the ability to make meaning of oneself and to reinterpret prior experiences in new ways (Ghosh et al., 2013; Kegan & Lahey, 2016).

PROMOTING DEVELOPMENT

The internal capacity to generate one's own views on the world, oneself, and relationships with others represents a significant developmental advance in meaning-making. The good news is that the development of these capacities can be promoted in adulthood (DeRue & Wellman, 2009; Ghosh et al., 2013; Helsing et al., 2008; Kegan & Lahey, 2016; Manners et al., 2004). Such programs were structured to modify and (in some cases) overturn long-held assumptions that limit participants' understanding as well as their actions. In the process, participants were typically engaged in a self-analysis of their own meaning-making. They were provided role-taking opportunities to practice new ways of acting followed by guided reflection and peer feedback. For example, research by Manners et al. (2004) demonstrated that providing experiences that are structurally disequilibrating, personally salient, interpersonal, and emotionally engaging can be effective in promoting ego stage advancement in adults. Critical to the relative success of these programs was the need for interventions that included deliberate challenge to existing assumptions. These challenges were intended to create the cognitive dissonance necessary to sufficiently perturb meaning-making.

These findings suggest that caregivers can help clients by clarifying arguments and by supporting or directing attention to arguments that present genuine cognitive conflict for the individual. Such discrepancies are designed to achieve an optimal balance that challenges the individual's existing mental structures while accommodating present experience. The caregiver acknowledges the client's reality, and then acts in ways that disrupt that structure. As an audience to their own presentation, clients must attempt to clarify the meaning of their arguments for this or that alternative. In efforts to restore some balance to the world as they know it, clients are supported in identifying what has changed, discovering what has been lost, and envisioning potential future actions.

A GROUPWORK APPROACH

Acknowledging that reality as one knows it is socially constructed is to recognize the dual nature of the self as defined in relationship to the other. Such a shift in thinking leads to a reconceptualization of individual counseling as but a subset of groupwork. Although groupwork is not a substitute for the "real" world, it serves as a real-world context for developing relationships. As argued previously, people make meaning within a social context that is informed by their current understanding of the past and their vision for the future. Participating in groupwork provides opportunities for members to be at their best in a supportive social setting while being challenged to work toward a preferred future. Groupwork can provide the kind of supportive social setting described in chapter 3 for both grieving the loss of the old self and rehearsing new behaviors.

In this way, groupwork provides a "holding environment" (see chapter 3) that will facilitate the member's efforts to restore some balance to the world as the member knows it. By encouraging group members to try out new roles and then examine their impact on others, the leader can promote consolidation of the new self and help establish a new equilibrium. Because reestablishment of equilibrium lessens the urgency toward change, this period requires different intervention styles than the period prior to intervention. In effect, interventions intended to challenge current understandings will necessarily be different than interventions intended to consolidate new understandings. Counselors should understand the fundamental differences between assimilation and accommodation and should know when to use each process most effectively.

Reginald Rose (1955) captured this tension between assimilation and accommodation brilliantly in his screenplay *Twelve Angry Men*. As the play opens, jurors are charged with determining whether a 19-year-old impoverished youth is guilty of having murdered his father. The judge instructs them that if found guilty, the defendant will receive a mandatory death sentence. The verdict, however, must be unanimous. At first, the evidence seems convincing: a neighbor testified she saw the boy stab his father from her window and through the windows of a passing elevated train. Another neighbor testified that he heard the boy threaten to kill his father and saw him running away. The boy has a violent past and had recently purchased a switchblade of the same type as was found at the murder scene. In a preliminary vote, all jurors vote guilty except juror Eight, who believes that there should be some discussion before the verdict is made.

Foreman. Okay. Eleven to one. Eleven guilty, one not guilty Now we know where we stand.

Three [rising to Eight]. Do you really believe he's not guilty?

Eight [quietly]. I don't know.

Seven [to Foreman]. After six days he doesn't know.

Twelve. In six days, I could learn calculus. This is A, B, C.

Eight. I don't believe it is as simple as A, B, C.

Three. I never saw a guiltier man in my life.

Eight. What does a guilty man look like? He is not guilty until we say he is guilty. Are we to vote on his face?

Three. You sat right in court and heard the same things I did. The man's a dangerous killer. You could see it.

Eight. Where do you look to see if a man is a killer?

Three [irritated by him]. Oh well! . . .

Eight [with quiet insistence]. I would like to know. Tell me what the facial characteristics of a killer are. Maybe you know something I don't know.

During their deliberations, the prejudices of each of the jurors are revealed. Having assimilated evidence presented during the trial into existing schemes, each explores the basis of their judgment of the youth's guilt. When challenged, each must confront the basis of their assumptions and the role these play in determining the guilt of the defendant. The following exchange between jurors Eight and Ten is typical.

Ten [to Eight]. I don't mind telling you this, mister. We don't owe the kid a thing, he got a fair trial, didn't he? You know what that trial cost? He's lucky he got it. Look, we're all grownups here, you're not going to tell us that we're supposed to believe him, knowing what he is. I've lived among them my whole life. You can't believe a word they say. You know that.

Nine [to Ten, slowly]. I don't know that. What a terrible thing for a man to believe! Since when is dishonesty a group characteristic? You have no monopoly on the truth!

After some efforts by other jurors to calm the situation, the discussion returns to the case.

Ten [loudly]. Just a minute. Here's a woman who's lying in bed and can't sleep. It's hot. Anyway, she wakes up and she looks out the window, and right across the street she sees the kid stick a knife into his father.

Eight. How can she really be sure it was the kid when she saw it through the windows of a passing elevated train?

Ten. She's known the kid all his life. His window is right opposite hers—across the el tracks—and she swore she saw him do it.

Eight. I heard her swear to it.

Ten. Okay. And they proved in court that you can look through the windows of a passing el train at night and see what's happening on the other side. They proved it.

Eight. Weren't you telling us just a minute or two ago that you can't trust them? That you can't believe them.

Ten [coldly]. So?

Eight. Then I'd like to ask you something. How come you believed her? She's one of them, too, isn't she?

Ten. You're a pretty smart fellow, aren't you?

In due course, all jurors are forced to accommodate their individual understandings of the events of the trial and accede to the decision to acquit the youth as "not guilty." Of course, all the jurors offer broad, wide-ranging assumptions that go far beyond the evidence or their charge as jurors. In turn, all are forced to face the loss of their unique assumptive worlds as their basic assumptions no longer make sense and there is no alternative way of seeing the world that will preserve their current beliefs in the face of a new reality. Such is the nature of drama and of real life as well.

Researchers have found that exposing individuals through group discussions to the reasoning of those who are more developmentally advanced can stimulate the development of more complex reasoning when the arguments are presented at a level just beyond the individual's current level of functioning (Rest et al., 1969; Torbert, 1994). By promoting self-reflection about past behavior, caregivers can help clients uncover the basic assumptions that have guided them to this point and construct a more viable system for explaining a new reality. Once having considered how someone came to behave in particular ways in the past, therefore, the caregiver shifts attention to a consideration of how the client will be different in the future. What the client will need to do to effect such a change and what the client will ask of others in the process are key issues to be addressed.

IN PASSING

I have attempted in this chapter to give you a glimpse across the landscape of events in what has been referred to as midlife. Of course, the middle for each of us is defined by our particular endpoints, one marked by our birth and the other as yet only speculation. Although the process of meaning-making can be put to different tasks by each of us, it is the form rather than the content of our efforts that has been the focus here. Any attempt to capture the full complexity of adulthood is doomed to the stereotyping, generalizing, and over-simplification that such enterprise demands, especially in a single chapter. Contrast the life trajectory presented in the normative mastery of life's tasks and the different experiences of a 15-year-old girl and a 47-year-old woman giving birth to her first child, or two biracial individuals who separately identify as African-American or Caucasian, or the career trajectories of fraternal twins, one of whom is male and the other female. Consider the different experiences of two brothers, 9 years apart in age, as they grow up in the same household subject to the same events.

A focus on these events rather than on the experience obscures what we mean when we talk of a meaningful life. I have chosen instead to focus on our efforts to make meaning of our unique experience, especially with others, in a world of our own making. As argued throughout, the inevitability of change challenges our understanding of that world and gives rise to what we experience as loss. Faced with recurring change in ourselves and the world of our understanding, we are engaged in a continual process of meaning-making, Therefore, it is critical to understand that loss is experienced in the moment of the event within the meaning-making system of the individual. In turn, these efforts lead to our personal understanding of the meaning of such change in our lives. In the chapter to come, we will explore more fully how meanings made such as acceptance, global beliefs, identity, causal understanding, or the significance of any event shape our experience as we face the challenges presented by life in the final third of our lives.

Chapter 8

Late(r) Life

Loss is nothing new to the person in late(r) life. As the previous chapters bear witness, our lives are punctuated with losses large and small, expected and unexpected, on-time and untimely, perceived and actual, necessary and situational. The journey to this point has faced the persistent challenge to make sense of the changes going on around us and, with each change, to experience a set of associated losses. As infants we came to make sense of temporary separations and unanticipated reunions with caregivers; as children we learned to deal with the disappointment that follows failed expectations; as adolescents we mourned our loss of innocence as we learned to integrate our own and others' expectations; as youth we learned to overcome our ambivalence about growing up; and as adults we have refined the personal narrative that accounts for, if not explains, the person we have been, are, and hope to become.

In each movement forward we have found ourselves once again as strangers living in a strange land. As Karp (1988) explains, the ageing person, like the stranger, "holds the distinctive position of being near and distant to a group at the same time" (p. 729). As we age, we become nearer and less distant as our place in this new age becomes more established. Unlike our experience with previous ages, however, the transition to late(r) life is strangely familiar. For the person in late(r) life, the experience of loss in all its forms has helped to establish a rich array of strategies for coping with our feelings. Anger, depression, frustration, anxiety, loneliness, resolve, regret, resignation, and hope have accompanied the myriad losses encountered over the course of life.

Although the road ahead has yet to be traveled, the person in late(r) life has been on this journey for a long time. Grandparents and close friends have died, jobs were lost and new jobs taken, children were raised and left home to start a new generation, the familiar roles of childhood gave way to more adult responsibilities, romances blossomed and relationships failed, basic appliances broke and an entire home was destroyed by fire, a favorite restaurant ran out of the "daily special" and a temporary unemployment lead to rationing and food stamps, the annual bout of the "flu" stands in stark contrast to a global pandemic, the hope for good weather this weekend stands beside the greater hope for a bright future for our children, the hysterectomy that ended childbearing, and the bumps and scrapes that brought tears in childhood pale in comparison to the prostate cancer diagnosis that says you'll die of something else first. Late(r) life brings its own set of challenges, most familiar, some unique, all fostered by change and accompanied by the loss that demands understanding.

It is an old theme by now: this need to develop a reliable self in a seamless continuity of attempts to make meaning of one's experience in an ever-changing world. Yet each loss has challenged the illusion of omnipotence and threatened to destroy the self so-carefully constructed. "Must I take the risk once more to build a self that can make better sense of this world? Can't I just hold on to the one I know and have now?" These are the persistent questions that frame our need for control—to establish an order to things of our own making. And once made, will that uniqueness be accepted by others? In advocating for a process of what Carlsen (1989) calls "creative ageing," she asks:

> Isn't "control" a question of the order of things—to have an order that one has created? A meaning, therefore, of one's own choosing? So, what if some of the basic therapeutic questions in working with ageing folks include the following: "How can we keep on finding uniqueness, a sense of participation in the order of things, and a place and time for intimacy and partnership? How do we handle the losses of our need fulfillments? How do we prepare ourselves early on for these losses as we find other needs to fulfill and other orders to maintain? (p. 81)

As in each previous epoch in our own development, the question is not how to avoid the losses we might experience. Instead, we need to experience the loss, name it, make meaning of it, and find a way *through* instead of *over* it. We need to construct a more competent self that can imagine a more reliable future. This mandate to make sense encourages us to both reinterpret and reimagine our experience and our actions in moving ahead. As well, there arises an even greater need in late(r) life to find meaning in the experience, to make life meaningful.

LOSS IN LATE(R) LIFE

According to the Centers for Disease Control (Arias & Xu, 2022), Americans can expect to live on average to age 76.3 for males and 81.4 for females. In the United States, the large cohort of Baby Boomers born between 1946 and 1964 will all be over 65 by 2030 when they are predicted to constitute 21 percent of the population (U.S. Census Bureau, 2018). The popular notion of life as ageing leads to referring to this period as "old age." As I write those words, I'm reminded of the unsolicited phone calls I receive daily offering to extend my car warranty. Like the contract that limits benefits to five years or 50, 000 miles, family genetics, gender, what accidents befall you in due course, how well you maintain your physical and mental health, where you live, how wealthy or educated you become, how stressful your life circumstances, employment conditions, and the like will determine in what condition and for how long you survive.

Despite medical advancements that have improved many aspects of healthcare, overall lifespan hasn't increased much. It's not that people live longer (i.e., lifespan), it's that more people are living longer (i.e., life expectancy). In effect, the longer you live, the longer you are expected to live but only up to a point and then, as it has been for millennia, you die. Unlike your car's warranty, however, there is no replacement guarantee, despite medical advances, for your worn-out parts should you fail to live as expected. Nonetheless, the cohort of Boomers is shaping our understanding of the "normal" ageing process in ways that challenge any easy characterization of life beyond age 65, hence the qualifier in the title as "late(r)."

Late(r) adulthood is typically considered to begin with retirement, although the specific age is being advanced beyond the customary 65 years and the status is complicated by the nature of one's employment. But typically, at age 65 and beyond, retirement represents one of the major losses in one's life and is one of the most complex. In a poignant reminder of the death of adolescence,

> Like high school graduation, [retirement] may be memorialized by the farewell dinner, speeches, and a gold watch, a peculiar symbol in view of the fact that time will probably be less structured than it was and its measurement less required; it may be a reaction formation or denial that time is limited, a replacement of time lost, a wish to the retiree of long time before death, or a memorial of time gone, like a grave marker. At any rate, in our inimitable cultural fashion the celebration conceals and denies the plethora of losses involved. The retiree is enjoined to be happy; the metaphor of retirement from work as retirement from life, or yet another step toward death, is blurred, but accounts for tears; the prospective retiree, on whom the last years of work may indeed hang heavy, are to metamorphoses sorrow to joy as a way of dealing with anticipatory mourning. Their turns will come. Meanwhile, those retiring are sailing forth into the sunset. (Weenolsen, 1988, pp. 301–302)

Additional losses of the period include increased physical restrictions in sensory areas and muscular flexibility, losses associated with disease, and the extra time spent attending to one's health. To these daily reminders of one's ageing, add the loss of self-image due to physical changes, the loss of companions and one's partner, the loss of home due to restricted finances or reduced physical or mental capacity, the loss of status that accompanies the loss of role expectations, the loss of "place" in an ever-changing landscape of technology, culture, and fashion, or the loss of self-esteem that comes from being ignored, excused, and excluded because no-one listens or even touches you anymore. Just reading this list is exhausting!

> Lucas was recently retired from his university position after some "fifty years behind the lectern," as he put it. Although 15 years my senior, we met occasionally as fellow travelers over lunch to "reinvent the world in our own images" and to speculate on the alternative futures we foresaw for ourselves and the world at large. This day's conversation took a different turn. Knowing of my academic interest in loss and taking the opportunity, as he put it, to "bootleg some therapy," we explored his growing apprehension about his life ahead and the impending reality of what he referred to as the "downsizing of my whole life." Facing a host of physical issues that included diminished hearing, reduced mobility, and a recent prostate cancer diagnosis, he drew no comfort from the physician's reassurance that these things are quite "normal at your age."
>
> "Living on a fixed income and having trouble keeping up physically," he began, "I'm aware I'm going to need to find a smaller home with more services and fewer responsibilities. I can't travel as much as I used to—no stamina—and I have to work twice as hard to do the simplest things that once seemed so easy," he said wistfully. "Just living is exhausting." And after a long pause, seeming to search for just the right summary, he explained, as if talking to himself, "It's an odd feeling, but it seems the world is shrinking around me . . . ," and as he paused, still searching for the right words, I added: "and it feels like you're not in control of your own future."
>
> "That's the damn irony of it, don't you think?" came the reply. "A life built on speculation and future building now reduced to consolidation and reflection. Mostly, I no longer feel in charge of my own life."

As explored in chapter 1, loss, especially for Americans, is about a loss of control—not just over the events in one's life but also a loss of one's self. In late(r) life, the losses that occasion changes in our sense of self are more and more due to forces beyond our control. Likewise, the new replacement self seems less and less of our own making. As captured by Weenolsen (1988), "I am all that I have been, but I am not now what I once was" (p. 301).

> Lucas and I talked for a while longer as we explored alternatives to the metaphor of a shrinking world and settled instead upon envisioning an ever-expanding universe. In such a world, he would no longer be confined to a life as he had known it and for which he felt responsible for its creation. Instead, he would

seek opportunities to expand his experiences. He would read more widely and develop new hobbies that expand rather than replace his current interests. He would explore his local community more thoroughly and nurture new and more diverse friendships. He decided to view his limited physical and financial resources as a challenge. He acknowledged the need to welcome the help offered by others as evidence of his worth. And he resolved to reevaluate what was important to him in shaping a "new and improved version" of himself.

A SHIFT IN COGNITION

Despite the general characterization of late(r) life as a period of significant cognitive decline, this statement doesn't mean that the greater proportion of older adults is necessarily impaired. Indeed, only 8.8 percent of adults aged 65 and older in the United States were identified as having dementia with an additional 18.8 percent estimated to be living with some cognitive impairment without dementia (Langa et al., 2017). Although dementia shows significant increases with age, it would be unfair to draw this period with such a broad brush. Instead, it may be more accurate to view individuals in this period as relying increasingly upon different cognitive abilities than previously.

Recall from chapter 6 that research supports the possibility of further development in adulthood, including continued advances in the ability to make meaning of oneself and reinterpret prior experiences in new ways. Research shows an increase in performance level during childhood and the highest levels of proficiency during adulthood. Results are ambiguous, however, as to whether these abilities decline with age, especially beyond age 65. It appears that cognitive development continues throughout adulthood but a decline in cognitive functioning can occur as one approaches the end of the lifespan.

Normal brain ageing results in an average decline in some cognitive functions (e.g., speed of thinking, working memory) across the population whereas other functions such as verbal ability are maintained (Ray & Davidson, 2014). Psychological distress, however, depends on how an individual perceives and responds to life events when these occur (McEwen, 1998). Age beyond 60 years does not appear to be strongly related to task performance when other variables are controlled, such as neurological decrement and social isolation. Notably, educational level, occupation, prior life experience, and a healthy lifestyle especially with loss, seem to provide an ameliorating effect absent any physiological impairment (Murman, 2015; Prince et al., 2014; Sinnott & Guttman, 1978).

The most common terminology used to describe which cognitive abilities change with age, and which do not, divides them into crystallized and fluid.

Fluid intelligence denotes the ability to acquire new knowledge such as used in problem-solving, whereas crystallized intelligence captures the amount of already acquired knowledge such as general knowledge of math, history, or vocabulary. Critically, there is an improvement in crystallized abilities until approximately age 60 followed by a plateau until age 80, while there is a nearly linear decline in fluid ability beyond age 20 (Murman, 2015, p. 113).

Openness to Experience, which reflects a person's willingness to explore, consider, and tolerate new experiences, ideas, and feelings, has been found to relate more strongly to crystallized intelligence than fluid intelligence (McCrae, 2004). People show increases in their level of Openness to Experience into their 20s and that level remains largely unchanged until the late sixties, with a modest decline thereafter (Terracciano et al., 2005). Moreover, Truluck and Courtenay (1999) found that older adults engage in more reflective learning, which involves the conscious consideration and analysis of beliefs and actions for the purpose of learning.

In sum, this research reveals that the ability to think logically and solve problems quickly in new situations tends to decline as adults age. Conversely, knowledge that comes from experience and prior learning increases over time. Reflection relies more on the consideration of past experience and multiple possible interpretations which help to create meaning. Coupled with the finding that Openness to Experience peeks in our 20s but is sustained through adulthood, this research points to the importance of developing habits of curiosity early in life. Taking interpersonal risks, reading widely, traveling broadly, and engaging in a variety of intellectually and culturally stimulating activities in one's 20s creates a rich storehouse of experience to draw upon for meaning-making as we age.

Because crystallized intelligence builds off the "edges" of what we already know, being Open early in one's life provides a much larger boundary of experiences from which to draw in dealing with the losses to be encountered in late(r) life. As adults age, they are encouraged to identify what interests them and why and build on what they already know in taking on new and challenging activities. When considering the role of assimilation and accommodation in late(r) life, people who are Open will find a greater variety of experiences to challenge their current understanding and press for accommodation. The greater use of crystallized intelligence, however, will necessarily draw upon a richer body of experience to which to assimilate new experience. Finding the right balance will depend on the richness of past experience and the demands made by any new experience. Not surprisingly, advanced levels of creativity and cognitive abilities among those in late(r) life show a high correlation with educational attainment and a richness of previous experience.

Taken as a whole, these results reinforce the importance of early experience and previous efforts to make meaning of loss on well-being in late(r) life.

Persons who are better educated, who have attained higher levels of cognitive development, who treat the stressors in their lives with optimism rather than as a threat, who are open to new experience, who are more socially engaged, and who have developed effective coping mechanisms are likely to continue to thrive beyond age 65, any major accident or disease notwithstanding.

A LIFE WELL-LIVED

From birth to death, each of us is engaged in the process of reviewing our lives. This life review is a process of rationalizing, reordering, or reconstructing reality in creating our own personal mythology. In considering where we have been, assessing where we are now, and evaluating lessons learned along the way, we position ourselves to imagine a better future. At its heart, this act of life review is a process of meaning-making. There is no fundamental difference between reflecting on one's past behavior and the construction, deconstruction, and reconstruction of a particular life event. Applied to the course of one's life in its entirety, the process is the same.

Recalling that meaning is made in the moment, however, means that the life we review at one juncture is not necessarily understood as the life as constructed at various other junctures along the trajectory of one's life. In essence, life review includes the review and reconstruction of previous reviews as we attempt to make better sense of our lives. Accordingly, life review is not necessarily a therapeutic technique, although it can be used in that way. Rather, it is essentially the process of making meaning, whether as children, adolescents, or ageing adults. Two life-long friends recall a humorous anecdote from their childhood, a retiree reflects upon the significant events in her career at a dinner in her honor, a high school teacher assigns students to write their own obituaries, a recovering alcoholic introduces himself at a meeting of Alcoholics Anonymous by telling "his story," a widow recounts the story of her marriage to a minister in an attempt to reconcile her husband's premature death with her faith in a benevolent god. All are forms of life review. All are intended to make sense of a life past, to re-examine current values and beliefs, and to reimagine the future going forward.

It is a process that is forever ongoing, often out of awareness, occasionally deliberate, and subject to constant revision. Whether a short introduction to a new acquaintance or a life-long review by a dying patient, life review serves this evaluative and reconstructive purpose. Applied to counseling, Carlsen (1991) lays out a set of goals for defining the value and meaning of life review in both individual and group process:

To assemble the pieces of personal history in a coherent story; to find some sort
of bridge between the interpersonal and the intrapersonal, between that which
is good and that which is not so good; to continue unto death the processes of
meaning-making which are at the heart of the human endeavor; to enter into
the mystery of life even as one allows for it, play with it, and incorporates it.
(pp. 164–165)

For those in late(r) life, reflection and self-evaluation take on a new importance. With a focus on the time remaining, planning one's future is as much
about completing the self-narrative that tells the story of a life past as it is
about shaping the form of a life ahead. The construction and reconstruction
of meaning that gives substance to our life's story now demands we bring the
story to a close.

The story that he has been telling of how he lived his life, smoothing out ruffled
relationships, adding significance where there was little, explaining a dubious
action in more acceptable terms, constructing and reconstructing meaning over
and over again to give self substance—all is drawing to a close and must be put
into final form, like the last draft of a manuscript. The time will come when no
changes can be made. The sense of personal urgency in this activity is not readily explainable unless we believe we will be held accountable in a new existence
or are concerned with the memory of ourselves that will remain in our children
and in the world. But this final life review, this construction of meaning and
integration into a finished self, must be performed. (Weenolsen, 1988, p. 304)

Whether in the telling and retelling of the story of a memorable Thanksgiving
dinner to someone newly introduced to one's family, in the writing of one's
biography, or in introducing oneself to peers as a member of a support group,
life review serves a special function in late(r) life. Beyond solving current
problems or formulating a better future, life review seeks to uncover the
meaning of life itself and whether one has lived faithful to one's values. Much
as hearing the stories of the Holocaust from her grandmother helped Ruth
(see chapter 6) to develop a sense of herself as capable, telling these stories
constituted their own life review for her Nannie. More than mere reminis-
cence, life review enabled Nannie to reflect on the meaning the Holocaust and
the loss of her family held for her. In telling and retelling her story, she could
demonstrate her appreciation for the significant courage displayed by her
family in their resistance and reinforce her gratitude for their foresight in saving her life. And in the process, she found meaning in her role to invigorate
her children and their children to act against discrimination and never forget.

COMING TO TERMS WITH THE SELF

No account of ageing can speak to all of us. Indeed, the meanings attributed to each age are a function of who you are at the time. In a comic routine variously attributed to George Carlin (Spatz, 2004), how we think about age changes over time:

> Do you realize that the only time in our lives when we like to get old is when we're kids? If you're less than 10 years old, you're so excited about ageing that you think in fractions. "How old are you?" "I'm four and a half!" You're never thirty-six and a half. You're four and a half, going on five! That's the key. So you BECOME 21, TURN 30, PUSH 40, REACH 50 and MAKE it to 60. Then a strange thing happens. If you make it over 100, you become a little kid again. "I'm 100 and a half!"

Instead of thinking of ageing as an event or status, like age, think of it as a natural process of change and loss over a lifetime that takes place on multiple levels, including the biological, psychological, and social domains. Note that this definition is devoid of such terms as progressive, persistent, decline, senescent, old, normal, or aged. Thus, one can talk of those in late(r) life as exhibiting a wide disparity in functioning. Because illness affects each person physically and mentally in different ways and at different rates, it results in different degrees of isolation depending upon the quality of social support. In the same way, we can talk of death and loss as events, while dying and losing are life processes of organizing experience and creating meaning. Understood in this way, dying is a kind of living and ageing is a kind of meaning-making. As we age, we are constantly living and dying and living again in efforts to make meaning of what went before and what lies ahead. But how one prepares for that event will be as unique as the history of losses one has encountered and the meanings made of those experiences.

A GOOD DEATH

All loss is about the illusion of our omnipotence and the story of our recreation in the face of change. Just as chapter 1 began, it is fitting here to remind ourselves that loss isn't something that happens to us as we live, rather it's living itself. Moreover, how we understand each loss is part of an ongoing evolution in the way in which we make meaning itself.

> I had the privilege of sitting with my father as he lay at home in his own bed dying of prostate cancer that had spread to his bones. The night before, we had

stayed up a bit "beyond his bedtime" as we swapped stories of our childhoods, searching for similarities and acknowledging the differences. His was a life filled with big losses: effectively leaving home at age 12 to gain his independence from an alcoholic father and an emotionally distant mother, working in a diner to support himself through the Great Depression, raising four boys against the backdrop of three wars that killed nearly half a million young men and women, building a business only to have it nearly destroyed by employees who stole his inventory, surviving a heart attack at age 61, and enduring the recurring hospitalizations of his wife (my mother) due to cancer over the decade that preceded her death.

He spoke almost reverently of her courage and of how his "near death experience" following his heart attack had given him a new perspective on his purpose in life: to care for the woman that had been his partner for more than 54 years. In review, he was comforted that they had raised four boys to become men of whom he could be proud and that they built a family business that allowed him to keep his promise that "you'll never go hungry." His was not the life he had imagined so often for himself, but it was a life he felt had led him to the future he foresaw in reuniting with his wife upon his impending death.

As I sat there, holding his mottled hand, black and blue from days on IV, I watched his eyes glaze over, his breathing become more measured, his face turn sallow, and his body become cool to the touch. "He is dying," I thought to myself. "If only he would die and relieve himself (or was it me?) of this misery." And as I listened—inhale, pause, exhale, pause, inhale, pause, exhale, pause, pause, inhale, pause, pause, pause—he was gone. I thought then and am reminded now, even as I write this, that we "come to life" and in death "we are gone." From where we come and to where we go are questions for philosophers and the faithful. For the moment, at least, I was comforted that his had been a "good death" (Meier et al., 2016).

Over the weeks that preceded his death, my father had been careful to put his affairs in order. A man who had lived his life secure in the illusion that he could surmount any loss, he revised his will, settled his financial affairs, said his "goodbyes" to old friends, made arrangements for a trusted neighbor to take his dog, and drew his sons and their families closer. He would die at home, under the watchful care of a hospice nurse who would manage his pain, feed, clothe, and bathe him when requested, and be informed by an advance directive that required, as he put it, "to let me just die in peace." He had his bed placed in the living room where he could keep an eye on the world around him and where he could continue to be a party to, if not a part of, the conversation. As he grew more and more comfortable with the inevitability of his death, he grew more accepting that he'd done all he could and that his was a life well-lived.

Much as there is no best way, only better ways, to live, there is no best way to die. Having gathered data from terminal patients, family members, and health care providers, Emily Meier (2016) and her colleagues, identified core themes associated with dying well. These themes are addressed to the difficulty Americans have in talking about death and their efforts to manage what is ultimately beyond their control. Communicating how one wants to die helps the dying person retain some sense of agency in the face of the inevitable. Maintaining a pain free status, having a choice in treatment preferences, and having a good relationship with health care providers can help in regulating the physical environment. Experiencing emotional well-being can be promoted by spiritual engagement and finding dignity in the dying process. Finally, having family present and saying goodbye offers opportunities for life review, having a sense of life completion, and realizing one's legacy. While the event of one's death marks the end of life, in dying as in living, we are faced with acknowledging the changes and making meaning of the reality that we are never more purely ourselves than when we lose.

IN PASSING

As universal as loss is to all of us, there is no right way to lose. What we lose, when we lose it, how we make sense of the loss, and what we do with the answers to these questions are as unique as the set of events that gave rise to the change that initiated this process of meaning-making. This chapter has brought the discussion of meaning-making and loss full circle from the birth of loss in infancy to the search for meaning in death.

As argued from the outset, loss is living itself. In each microsecond of our lives, we are engaged in this process of making meaning—of making sense of change and understanding the significance of any loss for our lives going forward. Guided by the illusion of our omnipotence in controlling recurring loss, we live out our lives against the ambivalence we hold toward death. As the popular song lyric goes: "Everybody wants to go to heaven, but nobody wants to die." Yet, in each moment of our lives, we are confronted by the possibility of our own death as we attempt to make sense of the changes going on around us. And in acknowledging any change, we must also acknowledge what is important to us. Because we only lose what we value, each loss defines who we are. Because each loss challenges who we are, we must take the risk to build a more competent self that can transcend that loss.

As presented, human development represents the course of our attempts to make sense of the changes going on around us. And further, how we understand each loss is part of an ongoing evolution in the way in which we make meaning itself. In this way, the process of living is the act of dying and being reborn, only to die again and again with each successive change. But death is not like those other change-initiating events. The loss of self we experience while living leads to its reconstruction in new and more viable forms. The event of our death, however, means the loss of our capacity to make meaning of the event itself. There is no resurrection, no life after death. From this per-spective, the event of our death represents the loss of meaning itself. What is left instead is the story of our efforts at living and the meaning our lives hold for those who remain.

Chapter 9

Caring for the Caregiver

In the span of just two years since the Centers for Disease Control reported the first U.S. laboratory-confirmed case of COVID-19 in the United States, more than 70 million cases were confirmed in the United States with an average of more than 400,000 new cases confirmed each day (New York Times, 2022). Tragically, COVID-19 has claimed the lives of more than 1,000,000 people in the United States since that report appeared (Donovan, 2022). As startling as these statistics are, they hardly capture the full scope of the losses that have resulted from a pandemic that shows no sign of abating. Throughout the world, we've all experienced losses large and small, but never everyone everywhere on the scale of a global pandemic that has no precedent in our lifetimes. The list is staggering.

LOSS IS EVERYWHERE

The pandemic has resulted in large unemployment numbers through illness or mitigation efforts to control the spread of the virus. The resulting economic recession has led to further job loss, which has fallen disproportionately on the low-wage workforce. This segment of the workforce tends to be far younger, more racially and ethnically diverse, and have completed less formal education than the displaced mid/high-wage workforce. The economic fallout from insufficient wages, unemployment, and supply chain issues has exacerbated an already fragile level of food insecurity and homelessness as the population of those living in poverty approaches 40 million. Fears of contracting COVID-19 have led to increased health risks for the most vulnerable populations. Consequently, there has been a 20 percent reduction in hospital admissions by people who need care but are avoiding hospitals or who can't easily access their doctor due to the high number of patients already under care (Birkmeyer, 2020). Most heartbreaking are the number of cases of family members who were unable to be with loved ones at the end of their lives.

Add to these conditions, the secondary losses occasioned by not seeing friends or family, the inability to participate in group sports, indoor recreation, theater, or concerts, not engaging in traditional ceremonies such as graduations, funerals, and weddings, postponing plans for travel, marriage, reunions, or pregnancy, the loneliness of sheltering at home, or the lack of human contact demanded by social distancing. And for the most vulnerable among us, cases of domestic violence and child abuse, suicides, homicides, and traffic fatalities all show increases attributed to the stress and isolation created by the pandemic. As public policy attempts to catch up with an emerging consensus on the cause, course, treatment, and cure for COVID-19, breakthrough cases raise doubts about the efficacy of any vaccine to end the pandemic. Add to all this loss, the stress and discord associated with public health measures such as face-coverings, vaccinations, and social distancing and you have all the ingredients for increased levels of anxiety, depression, and fatigue that have led to a global mental health crisis (Thornicroft, 2021; UNICEF, 2021).

IN SEARCH OF THE NEW NORMAL

Meaning-making has as its goal to construct a more stable and reliable understanding of a world that can be sustained in the face of recurring change. As such, meaning-making is as much about understanding the value of what has been lost as it is about predicting a viable future. At its core, meaning-making is fundamentally ambiguous in that it serves both to conserve the self as presented while envisioning a possible future self. This juxtaposition of preservation and recreation must necessarily be in balance if adaptation is to occur. To preserve one's sense of a coherent identity, it will be necessary to realize the proper balance between hope and resolve to be found through the "ambivalent testing of past and future" (Marris, 1986, p. 92). Understood in this way, meaning-making is fundamentally a conservative process by which future actions are premised upon past understandings applied to present circumstances. Although I've made the case repeatedly that the acknowledgment of change initiates this process of sense making, the outcome does not necessarily require significant change in the identity of the individual. More typically, each step forward continues a path shaped by prior attachments to people, events, and circumstances. In this way, the "new" normal grows out of and is an extension of the "old" normal. Whenever the familiar pattern of life has been disrupted by change, this process of adjustment will have to work itself out.

But what are we to make of losses that are so extensive as to be incomprehensible, so arbitrary as to defy prediction, so ambiguous as to go unresolved, so immediate as to preclude preparation? Under such conditions, loss loses all meaning. Prediction serves no purpose. And reflection finds no stable ground to rest on. This dissolution of definitional boundaries creates the ambiguity so many have experienced in this pandemic. This ambiguity arises from the anxiety created by an indeterminate future and the despair that comes from the loss of hope. The search for a new normal is the search for new boundaries within which meaning can be made that preserves past attachments in service of a more reliable future. Finding the new normal restores our faith that the past is not irrelevant, and that hope is not futile.

MARIO

No industry has been more affected by the pandemic than the restaurant business. The emergence of regulations to mitigate the effects of COVID-19 exposed long ignored deficiencies in health and safety, management practices, and working conditions. Faced with the added insecurity of contracting a deadly disease, more restaurant employees are quitting than in any other industry (Bureau of Labor Statistics, 2022, February). Having experienced significant reductions in the number of patrons, inadequate responses to rapidly changing regulations, and an uncertain supply chain, in addition to the inability to retain employees, nearly 17 percent of U.S. restaurants (i.e., 110,000 establishments) had closed permanently by the end of the first full year of the pandemic (National Restaurant Association, 2022).

Mario grew up in the restaurant business. As long as he could remember, he had been hanging around Gino's—the pizza parlor his grandfather had founded after emigrating from Italy following World War II. Putting out trash before school, setting up tables each afternoon, and getting to pull pies from the oven on weekends when business picked up, he became as much a fixture of the place as the picture of its founder that hung proudly above the entrance. By high school, he had a regular job out front, taking orders and charming customers with his optimism and trademark smile. He skipped an opportunity to go to college, preferring to continue the family tradition now carried on by his "papa." Mario dreamed of the day that Gino's would be his—the third generation "padrone." Then he'd start his own chain of restaurants and call them "Mario's Too." That time came sooner than he had imagined. His father suffered a massive heart attack that left him paralyzed on one side and confined to his bed until his death several years later. Now married and with twin daughters, Mario worked 14-hour days building a business that grew to three locations that employed more than 30 staff serving the "best pie money can buy." That was 2020.

Then his 63-year-old mother took ill and was hospitalized with what at first was diagnosed as pneumonia. Today we know better. As her lungs deteriorated, her breathing accelerated and she struggled to get enough air, gasping for hours on end. She said it felt like she was being smothered by a thousand bees stinging inside her chest. Properly diagnosed with COVID-19, she was placed in isolation. The hospital enacted infection control measures to identify and isolate patients, clean and disinfect surfaces, restrict visitors, socially distance staff, and require the wearing of personal protective equipment. In turn, her anxiety cycled with depression as she was visited by anonymous ICU nurses, dressed like beekeepers, who came to administer the medications and monitor the ventilator and heart-lung machine intended to ease her pain and sustain her life. There in the hospital, unable to enjoy the company of her family, she would die alone in the company of caring strangers.

Hospitals were not alone in their response to what came to be widely recognized as a significant public health risk. Government officials warned Americans to practice social distancing, public gatherings of more than 10 people were discouraged, air travel was restricted, holiday parades were canceled, sporting tournaments were postponed or canceled altogether, and curfews were imposed on bars, restaurants, gyms, and movie theaters. Schools were closed and took to online learning as caregivers were thrust into managing daycare and home schooling. Conflicting scientific reports, mass distribution of misinformation, and uneven public health responses complicated an already complex situation.

In response, Mario plunged himself into his work. Further isolating himself from his family, he protected himself from grieving the loss of his mother and from facing the devastating impact these regulations were having on his business. Seating was limited, tables were spaced farther apart, staff and customers alike were masked, and an outdoor seating area was hastily erected on the sidewalk. More and more customers preferred to order out, however, and then quit coming at all. Staff regularly reported in sick or resigned out of caution that they might become ill themselves or infect their families. Despite his efforts, he was forced to close first one and then the next, and finally his original location. Although he received some federal financial assistance, he found his staff, mostly women with small children of their own, were reluctant to return to work. He felt trapped in a restaurant that wasn't making enough money to support his family despite its outward success and whose income he relied on to pay the debts he had acquired in expanding the business. And then, in the cruelest of blows, Mario's wife died alone in a hospital ICU of a brain aneurysm as the result of a fall the night before. Now 41, Mario was left to raise two seven-year-old daughters without the support of either parents, a partner, an accessible community of friends, or a viable source of income. Mario was now a single parent responsible for the care of two school-aged children.

Such is the nature of ambiguous loss: the lack of a clear understanding of the circumstances of his mother's death by a novel disease; the sudden and unexpected death of his wife that undermined prediction; the unresolved feelings of guilt for not being with his mother or his wife at the end; the lack of closure in being unable to celebrate their deaths in public ceremonies with friends and family; and the anxiety and depression created by the rapid change in treatment options that offered hope and then despair. Compounding his unresolved grief were similar ambiguous losses related to his failing business. He was unable to retain his staff who struggled with their own losses at home. The rapidity of constantly changing government regulations made any adjustment temporary. And the social isolation from friends and co-workers left him losing confidence in the future. These losses are ambiguous because they are unexpected, caused by forces beyond reason, and for which there are no rituals nor even language to acknowledge the loss of control we feel over our lives.

One would not have been surprised had Mario ended his own life in despair. But the optimism that had guided his previous success found renewed energy in the hope he saw in his children and the debt he felt he owed to the family that had launched his career. In homage to his mother, he returned to the church he had forsaken as a teenager and sought the guidance of the parish priest. The Father acknowledged Mario's pain as both extraordinary and normal and encouraged Mario to "stay the course." As a first step in normalizing Mario's grief, the Father arranged for Mario and the twins to visit the parish cemetery where his wife and mother were buried. There, among the headstones that marked their graves and those of three generations of his family, Mario wept for the first time. Able to bring some closure at last to the finality of their deaths, he was also able to re-establish the continuity with his father and grandfather that had long shaped his restaurant dreams.

In the days and weeks to follow, the Father helped him learn how to share his grief appropriately with his children. The Father stressed the need to provide accurate information and the importance of maintaining healthy family routines. Mario learned to be patient with the twins' persistent questioning about the permanence of death while assuring them that he would be there to protect them. In each exchange, he tried to help them put their feelings into words in their ongoing efforts to make meaning of what seemed meaningless. As audience to his own conversation, Mario grew to appreciate the power in his own story, which connected him to those he had lost and to his children in a continuity of care. He joined a group of parents online who were home-schooling their children and, as vaccines became more readily available, he felt more confident in reaching out to similarly vaccinated and masked neighbors for social distancing and catered meals. The Pod Squad, as they called themselves, became the touchstone for exploring his natural feelings of frustration and his concerns about his children's adjustment, as well as sharing helpful strategies and stories of hope.

As people began to return to work and school, Mario was confronted by the decision to reopen his businesses. He reviewed the significance losing his restaurants might have and the role they had played in shaping his life. He realized that it was the opportunity to share in his family's traditions and to build something of value that had guided his efforts. Having assessed his values around work and home, he believed there was no going back to those pre-pandemic days of long hours at work, away from his family, and without the immense satisfaction he found in raising his daughters. He was a very different person from whom he had been 18 months earlier and he would now have to navigate a "new normal." He found a buyer who shared his dream of owning a restaurant and used the money from the sale to pay down his debts and ensure support for his family as he reimagined his future. Encouraged by his success in building a life with his children, he applied for student loans and enrolled in college. Mario would become a teacher.

SARA

The COVID-19 pandemic has been the single deadliest acute public health crisis in American history (Treglia et al. 2021, p. 6). As the number of COVID-19 cases accelerated, healthcare systems became overwhelmed. Great psychological pressure was exerted on nurses, in particular, those who are responsible for the care of critically ill patients. Registered Nurses comprise the largest sector of the healthcare workforce in the United States (American Association of Colleges of Nursing, 2019). Despite the growing demand for their services, nurses have been leaving the profession in record numbers. In a particular irony, nurses have quit their positions in response to high levels of stress created by staffing shortages that have eroded the quality of their work life, the quality of patient care, and the amount of time nurses can spend with patients (American Association of Colleges of Nursing, 2020). With the onset of the pandemic, nurses were confronted by a disease with no known cure, record numbers of hospitalizations, fears for their own safety, insufficient staffing, and the anxiety created by hastily enacted safety protocols and a lack of personal protective equipment.

Rather than helping patients recover from acute disease or disability, nurses who work with terminally-ill patients in the Intensive Care Unit (ICU) focus on the needs of dying individuals and their relatives (Martens, 2009). Although unrestricted visitation from family members into the ICU had been shown to improve patient care (American Association of Critical-Care Nurses, 2016), that practice ended with the pandemic. Strict safety protocols that changed almost daily were enacted to limit admission strictly to necessary medical personnel. To further reduce the number of people in patients' rooms, nurses took on tasks that licensed nursing assistants would typically do, such as feeding or assisting patients in personal hygiene. Not allowing visitors made the unit quieter and less chaotic. It also limited communication, decision-making, and family support at critical moments in patients' lives. Nurses became creative in identifying workarounds to meet the needs of patients, families, and the health care team. As one nurse explained,

I cared for a dying patient during the last hours. The family was not present . . . I found the patient's phone and figured out how to play music . . . I was the only reminder in the room that this was a person with a life . . . now facing death.. alone except for me. (Bosek et al., 2021, as cited in Franz, 2021, para. 8)

In a heartbreakingly real video (Stockton & King, 2021), we are taken inside a hospital ICU to see the work first-hand of nurses engaged in caring for the sickest of pandemic patients. Until viewing this video, few could imagine what goes on in such a depressing place. There we are introduced to Sara Reynolds, a career nurse who takes us inside the operation of the ICU and into the hearts and minds of those who work in this windowless room filled with death. These nurses work in 12-hour shifts or longer providing critical care to two or even three patients depending upon available staff. As Sara described the work, "Because they're so critical, they need continuous monitoring. . . . Physically it's exhausting. We're just running. We don't have time to eat or drink or use the restroom."

In a related study by Bosek et al. (2021), nurses described the transformation of their experience over months of the pandemic from a rollercoaster ride to a trudging marathon with no clear or recognizable end in sight. "I'm in this marathon, I'm tired, I'm trying to take care of myself, I want to care for people, but it's harder, different and takes more effort" (cited in Franz, 2021, para. 16). With their patients dying regularly, these nurses are confronted daily with the prospect, as well as the reality, of death.

Sara wonders with each caring act if this will be the last thing she ever does for this patient. "It just breaks my heart when I hear families saying 'goodbye.' . . . And I talked to family and let them know that we have done everything that we can. There's nothing more that we can do. . . . If I'm there while someone is passing, I always hold their hand. I don't want somebody to die alone. That's something that brings me peace. . . . I always wonder, are they still going to be there when I get to work? On my mind when I get home, are they going to make it through the night? What's sad is when I go back, those beds will be full. They'll have somebody else there just as sick with another long stretch of a few weeks ahead of them before it's time for their family to make that decision to let them die."

In the indeterminacy of their work life, these nurses experienced a dissolution of the boundaries that united them with other healthcare workers and delimited their relationship with their patients. In their search for a new normal, new boundaries dissolved with each new protocol only to be replaced the next day with yet another reality. Unable to find a new normal, the past became increasingly irrelevant as their hope of transcending the chaos waned.

They turned to one another as the most reliable (and obviously available) source of comfort and strength. Sara explains:

> I'm getting older now, and there's all these new young nurses coming out and I feel like a mom to all of them. They have kids at home, doing online school. And I think, gosh, they haven't even been able to check on their kids to see how they're doing. . . . We're the only ones to know what we're going through. I don't really want to tell my family about everything because I don't want them to feel the same emotions that I feel. I don't want them to know that I carry that burden when it—that it is a lot. I'm mom. I'm strong. I can do anything. And I don't want them to see that.

> Nurses are justifiably proud of the work they do. Despite being among the most highly respected of professionals (Reinhart, 2020), nurses fear they can't keep up the standards for honesty and ethical behavior that earned them that respect. As Sara put it: "I can't give the quality of care that I normally would give. It's absolutely dangerous. That's demoralizing because we care. We're nurses."

This disconnect between knowing the ethically correct action to take but being constrained from taking it is the essence of moral distress (Henrich et al., 2016). Moral distress profoundly threatens our core values, which are at the heart of what it means to make meaning. Although the causes vary among individuals, the perfect storm of end-of-life care, inadequate staffing, challenging team dynamics, and duty conflicting with safety concerns explains why moral distress is so prevalent among nurses caring for critically ill patients.

> This tension between the tenets of ethical practice that define who she has been and the person she fears she may have to become under trying circumstances tested Sara's core identity: "I've always wanted to be a nurse. It's what I've always wanted to do. And these past couple months, it's definitely made me question my career choice." The injustice of being put in this collision of values by forces she viewed as largely beyond her control gave rise to unfamiliar feelings in a person for whom compassionate care is central to her professional identity. Sara explains: "I think like many health care workers, I'm angry a lot. And my faith in humanity has dwindled. How can you think this isn't a real thing? How can you think that it's not a big deal?"

> As the pandemic has continued, many nurses have noted a similar struggle to not be angry with people they perceived as making things more difficult for them. Physician Ashley Montgomery-Yates says she used to get angry when so many unvaccinated patients showed up in her ICU. "We have to convince them in order to save ourselves," she said. "Because the strokes, and the heart attacks, and the cancers—they're all still coming in. If they don't get vaccinated," she asks, "how am I ever going to get my hospital back?" (Armstrong, 2021, p. 15).

Even more disruptive was the sense that people are nervous being near them for fear they will catch COVID-19 while expecting nurses to take care of them if they become ill. How are we to make sense of this paradoxical behavior?

This ambivalent testing of past and future must be resolved if the individual is to reconcile any loss. In times of extreme stress caused by seemingly random or capricious forces, people tend to rely upon others who share their strong sense of group identity and whose behavior is governed by adherence to a deeply held set of core beliefs (Hawkins et al. 2018). In dealing with the persistent and wide-scale ambiguity of loss associated with the pandemic, the airing of one's grievances became for many the only meaningful activity for grieving itself. One of the distinctive features of this group behavior is its ability to institutionalize ambiguity. Unless and until some continuity with the past can be retrieved to build a more reliable future, membership in a community of the similarly grieved helps in understanding the everyday demands of living. Membership protects the individual from confronting the ambiguity of unacknowledged losses and provides a substitute for their own uncertain identities.

It may not be too much to understand the experience of ICU nurses, as conforming to these forces for identification. Although the popular image portrays them as caring and trusted, nurses aren't viewed as influential or autonomous providers. Overwhelmingly, nurses have identified a lack of control and uncertain clinician status as the leading causes of distress for them (Shechter et al., 2020). Isolated by the very protocols intended to protect them and constrained by the ethical standards for practice and their own identity within the profession, two-thirds of nurses surveyed have considered leaving the field (American Association of Critical-Care Nurses, 2021). Burnout, workload, COVID-19 associated stresses, and the perception that the hospital prioritized the organization's financial outlook over the best interests of the nursing staff and patient care were found to be associated with the intent to reduce hours or leave. In contrast, feeling valued was strongly associated with lower odds of reducing hours or leaving (Sinsky et al., 2021).

For those nurses remaining, a change in behavior would be necessary if they were going to meet the needs of the patients, co-workers, family, and neighbors who depended upon them for physical and psychological support. And so, physical exercise and self-care became the primary means for nurses to deal with stress and resolve the tension between preserving their idealized sense of self and accepting the realities of their practice (Shechter et al., 2020). As one of Bosek et al.'s (2021) nurses advised: "Self-care is a must. . . . take time to take care of yourself. At the end of your shift, reflect, take some deep breaths, and move on. Remember that you are doing your best and that is enough."

KENYATTA

Eighteen months into the pandemic, 3.5 million teachers and support staff found themselves pressed to return to face-to-face instruction in the classrooms of the 14,000 school districts across America. Teachers spent substantial portions of the previous schoolyear mastering the technological and logistical challenges of teaching in hybrid and online classes. Returning to school meant teachers were faced with restoring the educational trajectories of nearly 1.7 million public school students. Unlike the multitrillion-dollar relief packages that supported small businesses at risk, built field hospitals, sourced protective equipment, developed and distributed vaccines, and put national regulations in place, state and local governments now seemed helpless in enacting similar measures in the nation's schools. As getting moms and dads back to work became a national priority, the responsibility fell to teachers to save the economy. As one high school art teacher captured the issue:

> It's not on our backs how the economy does. But every time there's a crisis in our communities, in some ways, there's the perception that we're supposed to be the ones handling it. Are we going to get the materials we need? Are there going to be enough masks? That's going to cost more money that we don't have. (Reilly, 2020, Fertig, para. 2)

The disparities teachers faced in the fall of 2021 were not new, however. As in so many other industries, COVID-19 accelerated long-standing grievances related to pay, job responsibilities, and public respect that led to the largest drop in public education jobs ever recorded in the federal data (Bureau of Labor Statistics, 2022, March). These staffing challenges didn't stop at the teacher's desk, however. The Boston Public Schools Superintendent reported consistently having a 20 percent job vacancy in food and nutrition services in addition to shortages of more than 100 bus monitors and approximately 30 bus drivers on any given day (Cassellius, 2022).

As well, the pandemic negatively affected the academic growth of children in ways that have visited multiple losses with likely devastating consequences for years to come. Emerging evidence from the Office for Civil Rights (2021) shows that COVID-19 appears to have deepened the impact of disparities in access and opportunity facing many students of color in public schools. Technological and other barriers made it harder for these children to stay engaged in virtual classrooms. Many children lost access to school-based services and to affirming student organizations and supportive peers, teachers, and school staff. The risks of sexual harassment, abuse, and violence from household members as well as intimate partners were heightened as well as online harassment from peers and others, especially for females and gender non-conforming students. Add to these tragic circumstances the deaths that left more than 167,000 U.S. children under the age of 18 years suffering the loss of a parent or other in-home caregiver to COVID-19 (COVID Collaborative, 2021).

Children have always brought these vestiges of trauma from home with them to school, but not on this scale. In a profession whose core value is caring, now every student, every teacher, and every staff member was actively grieving some loss that demanded attention. Teachers' identities—the personal narratives they tell about themselves and that others tell about them—are shaped by how well they see themselves as caring for their students. Facing the "multiplicity of competing and conflicting forces trying to define educational reality" (Craig, 2002, p. 199), teachers have always found security from these intrusions in "their" classrooms with "their" students doing "their" best to improve the lives of every child. With COVID-19, the work of teachers is once again being defined by others. The debate over reopening schools and the battles over pandemic-related policies on masking and vaccines put parents and politicians at odds with school leaders. In turn, teachers found themselves in the impossible position of weighing their commitments to caring for other people's children against their commitments to care for themselves and their loved ones.

This is the world Kenyatta Reed (Long, 2021) faced as she returned to her fourth-grade classroom in Jackson, Mississippi in the fall of 2021. "It's very, very different. . . . Every day I'm worried," she says. "Standing at the board, I feel my anxiety rising each day. I know the risks we're taking. . . . This isn't normal, it may be our new normal, but none of it feels normal." (para. 1–2, 10)

Kenyatta, mother of two public school students, isn't alone in her anxiety. With one in three teachers responsible for the care of their own children while teaching (Steiner & Woo, 2021), educators and parents alike are feeling uneasy about the impact it can have on their students, themselves, and their own children and families. "We need to be vigilant about keeping the students safe from the virus, " Kenyatta says, "which on top of the normal workload of educating them, is a lot" (para. 10). . . . "We have gloves, masks, Lysol, whatever PPE we need, my school has, but our emotions are all over the place" (para. 13). With all her family members out of the house at school or at work, she is anxious they will be in contact with others who are infected with COVID-19 and bring it home with them. Her fears are quite real given the fact that 4,500 students state-wide tested positive for COVID-19 and more than 20,000 were under quarantine as school began. Although she and two co-workers were vaccinated, nearly 1,000 teachers or staff members state-wide tested positive.

Like so many caregivers on the front lines of the pandemic, teachers found themselves under enormous stress from the uncertainty about the consequences of the pandemic, work overload, physical distancing from social support networks, conflict and role ambiguity, an inadequate physical environment, the use of new technologies, and difficulties combining work and family (Steiner & Woo, 2021). Together, these conditions created the perfect environment for the burnout teachers experience when they are responsible for things they have no authority over. Add to these stressors, the public and political calls for new laws to curtail instruction related to race, racism, and gender, and it's no surprise that a survey of K-12 teachers found nearly half were "very likely" or "fairly likely" to leave the profession in the next two years (Merrimack College, 2022).

> Kenyatta felt grateful for the attention given to her by fellow teachers and her principal. The state teachers' association kept in contact with emails and webinars about handling stress. And she came to rely on a colleague to take over her class when she needed a break or the opportunity to collect herself rather than break down in class. In summary, she remarked, "I think we all need to know we have a partner in the building who has your back, who you know is going through this with you, that mentally, you have each other" (para. 17).

The pandemic, by its persistence and uncertainty, has made ambiguous loss a mainstay of daily life. In a world where past experience is a poor guide for future action, stress overwhelms our efforts to make meaning. Stress challenges who we are and threatens who we can become. This idea of the self as a meaning-making system brings this chapter full circle to the statement that *loss is living itself* with which this book began. Over the previous eight chapters, I've charted the regular and predictable changes we undergo in which former losses are resolved and the possibility of experiencing new ones is created. But what meaning are we to make of change that overwhelms rather than merely challenges our efforts at understanding? What are we to do to relieve the stress we feel from having lost our way? What meaning can we make of events when the fundamental assumptions at the core of our identities repeatedly fail us? And how will we regain equilibrium when the identities we have become, and to which we are now committed, go out of balance again?

SELF-CARE

Clients enter counseling with meaning systems that have somehow failed to support their efforts to make sense. In caring for others, therefore, one should begin by trying to understand how they make meaning of the world as they experience it. It's in this place between an event and our reaction to it that we attempt to make meaning of the loss that change creates. Any attempt to understand another's world, however, risks the possibility of losing one's self in the process. Part of the pre-flight instruction on any commercial airline directs passengers who are traveling with a child or someone who requires assistance "to secure your mask on first, and then assist the other person." The significance of this directive lies in the reality that you can't be much help to others if you don't take care of yourself first.

Entering this place where meaning itself is made is an act of courage by the caregiver who risks being changed by the change sought in the other. The physician who must help a patient receive a cancer diagnosis, the veteran who consoles an active-duty soldier following surgery to remove a damaged limb, the mother who must explain the unexpected death of her husband to their children, or the school nurse who must make sense of a child's report of unwanted touching by a custodial adult, all take the risk to be changed by these encounters. Caregivers are challenged to help others explore the meaning of any loss while not making the other's pain their own. As we have seen with children, striking this balance is particularly important in dealing with losses that are personally distasteful. Caring for others also risks being visited by your own unresolved issues related to loss.

It bears repeating that such encounters embody the essential nature of loss: the challenge to see the world differently and the realization that the world will be different only if we change. As psychologist Michael Mahoney (1995) explains the risk:

> Those efforts toward knowing, in turn, require that counselors be capable of encouraging an intimate level of self-description and self-presentation on the part of clients. Some of these descriptions and presentations are difficult to follow or painful to witness. They may include emotionally intense and vividly detailed reports of abuse, cruelty, injustice, and tragedy. Not only are such life stories painful to hear, but the emotional pain of the client in the process of relating them can also be formidable. And just as the words and "voice" of the counselor go with clients into their lives outside and after psychotherapy, so do their words, their stories, and their heart-wrenching tears remain with the counselor through his or her career. (Mahoney, 1995, p. 387)

In confronting others, one makes oneself vulnerable to change. By taking the risk to build a more stable relationship, one risks losing the present relationship, however ineffective or incomplete. In exploring how others create their experiential worlds, caregivers can increase both their own and others' awareness of the limitations and opportunities present in their current understandings. Recognizing that we cannot escape our own constructed reality, however, caring is nothing less than an attempt to create the conditions for such exploration.

Although we cannot as caregivers bridge the gap between our own and another's experience, we are guided by our faith in our ability to facilitate greater understanding. In caring for another, therefore, the best we can hope for is a reliable, rather than a verifiable, road map to guide our interactions. If we accept we can never really know the truth of what happens, then truth lies in the intersubjectivity of the truths we each bring to understanding the world. This view of reality as a self-constructive activity means that caregivers should try to understand how people make meaning of their personal experience and of the losses that attend living in a constantly changing world. Significantly, this development of greater understanding takes place within a social context that has the potential to change the caregiver as well.

Because we can never fully understand the ambiguity that attends to facilitating new ways of balancing old and new ways of experiencing, this approach has no specific direction nor any fixed outcome. Instead, this approach is an organic, collaborative, and dialectical process of endless redescriptions of the world by which people with different beliefs and perspectives develop mutual understanding. This approach demands a high tolerance for ambiguity—the capacity to balance contradictions in dealing with uncertainty, unpredictability, conflicting directions, and multiple demands. Critically, tolerance for ambiguity has become a defining characteristic for caregivers to operate effectively in navigating the uncertain landscape of a global pandemic.

This journey begins with acknowledging that you are living in a very different time. As Mario, Sara, and Kenyatta steered their ways through the maze of changes in their work and home lives, each was challenged to re-envision life as they had known it. Each was forced to manage their expectations of themselves, and, in turn, what they could expect of others. In such periods of discovery, caregivers are advised to accept that they will make mistakes. Such is the nature of ambiguity. Try to become more flexible in your expectations. Forgive yourself for not being your "best you" while accepting you are doing the "best you can." Build up a tolerance for the annoying behavior of others and extend this courtesy to others for not being at their best as well. Above all, let go of the guilt you feel for not doing all that you can.

At its heart, the pandemic speaks to a recurring fear that the selves we have worked so hard to construct may be overwhelmed at any moment by forces beyond our control. Re-establishing control, therefore, becomes a central task in managing stress. Because you are always making meaning, monitor your thinking and its effect on how you feel and how you behave. Recognizing that meaning-making serves both to make sense of the past and forecast a viable future, accept that everything that could happen won't happen and that the worst thing you can imagine is the thing least likely to happen. Recognize that the stress you feel is in direct proportion to the lack of control you experience. Setting new boundaries will bring some order to the chaos and help to make the ambiguity more manageable if not also predictable.

Although meaning-making is essentially a cognitive function that distinguishes us as humans, we are also fundamentally biological organisms. Just as what we think, feel, and believe can affect our physical health, what we do with our physical bodies has an impact on our mental health. Managing the ambiguity, therefore, will also mean gaining control over our behavior. Create daily routines for exercising, eating well-balanced meals, maintaining personal hygiene, and taking time-out from worry in a place safe from stress.

Changing your behavior also means creating new routines and the habits that flow from them. Making plans will help you feel more in control, including some things you'd like to do when the pandemic subsides. Learn to pace yourself by breaking up the stress into manageable chunks. Limit the amount of "breaking news as it happens" in your life to an amount that makes you feel informed without supporting your anxiety and heightening your stress. And reduce the clutter in your life by getting rid of things you no longer need. Postpone or eliminate tasks that are more than you can take on right now. In particular, drop relationships that don't help you grow as a person.

Because we live in a social world of changing perspectives, what we know is constructed through experience, especially with others. We are, after all, social beings who derive our identities by and through our associations with others. Although we bring our own reality to addressing life's problems, creating new meaning structures in discourse with others permits experience to be considered from multiple perspectives. Recall that Mario, Sara, and Kenyatta all found their relationships with friends and colleagues to be a critical ingredient in managing stress and validating their experience. Lacking any continuity with the past that could be used to build more reliable futures, they found membership in a community of the similarly grieved helped protect them from confronting the ambiguity of unacknowledged losses and provided a substitute for their own uncertain identities.

Working together to determine the most workable course of action under present conditions offered them hope for shaping their experiences tomorrow. Moreover, they found family and friends to be significant forms of support who valued their contributions and provided tangible evidence of their success. For Mario, talk therapy and attending a support group run by a qualified professional offered similar benefits with the added measure of retaining his anonymity. In closing I am reminded of the advice I so often offer to doctoral students and clinicians early in their careers: "When in doubt, seek supervision." Similarly, I encourage you as a caregiver to seek out family and friends and build a community of like-minded colleagues who can support your efforts to make meaning of the ambiguity we face together.

IN PASSING

There will be no returning to the "old normal." Instead, we are challenged to grieve its loss. We must recognize what part of our past we want to bring along into the present as we construct a more reliable self for navigating an uncertain future. The magnitude of ambiguous loss experienced during the pandemic has made it difficult to grieve when so many of those losses remain unrecognized and when the pandemic itself has yet to end. What this means going forward is that there will be recurring challenges to understanding our world as each of these losses is experienced, perhaps for the first time. The meaning we make of these losses will be critically important to our efforts to construct a more stable and reliable understanding of that world. For now, understand that you are already changed and that you will continue to change with each new understanding. In the meantime, be patient with yourself as you contemplate what you want your new life to be. Build on your achievements as a strength of character and recognize your resilience in meeting the demands of each day anew.

Bibliography

American Association of Colleges of Nursing. (2019, April 1). *Fact sheets: Nursing fact sheet.* Retrieved from www.aacnnursing.org/News-Information/Fact-Sheets/ Nursing-Fact-Sheet

American Association of Colleges of Nursing. (2020, September). *Nursing shortage.* Retrieved from www.aacnnursing.org/News-Information/Fact-Sheets/Nursing -Shortage

American Association of Critical-Care Nurses. (2016). Family visitation in the adult intensive care unit. *Crit Care Nurse, 36*(1), 15–18.

American Association of Critical-Care Nurses. (2021, September 21). *Hear Us Out Campaign reports nurses' COVID-19 reality.* Retrieved from www.aacn.org/ newsroom/hear-us-out-campaign-reports-nurses-covid-19-reality

American Psychological Association. (2018). *Stress in America: Generation Z.* Washington, DC: Author. Retrieved from www.apa.org/news/press/releases/stress /2018/stress-gen-z.pdf

American Psychological Association. (2021). *Stress in America: Stress and decision-making during the pandemic.* Washington, DC: Author. Retrieved from www.apa.org/news/press/releases/stress/2021/decision-making-october-2021.pdf

Arias, E., & Xu, J. (2022, March 22). United States life tables, 2019. *National Vital Statistics Reports, 70*(19). Hyattsville, MD: National Center for Health Statistics.

Armstrong, D. (2021, December 15). Unvaccinated Covid patients push hospital systems past the brink. Bloomberg. www.bloomberg.com/graphics/2021-covid-surge -shows-overwhelming-cost-of-being-unvaccinated-america/

Arnett, J. (2000). Emerging adulthood: A theory of development from the late teens through the twenties. *American Psychologist, 55*, 469–480.

Arnett, J., Kloep, M., Hendry, L., & Tanner, J. (Eds.). (2011). *Debating emerging adulthood: Stage or process?* New York, NY: Oxford University Press.

Attig, T. (2011). *How we grieve: Relearning the world* (rev. ed.). New York, NY: Oxford University Press.

Bakhtin, M. M. (1981). *The dialogic imagination: Four essays* (M. Holquist, Ed., & C. Emerson & M. Holquist, Trans.). Austin, TX: University of Texas Press.

Baldwin, J. M. (1902). *Social and ethical interpretations in mental development.* New York, NY: Macmillan. (Original work published 1897)

Balk, D. (2014). Dealing with dying, death, and grief during adolescence. New York, NY: Routledge.

Basseches, M. (2005). The development of dialectical thinking as an approach to integration. *Integral Review, 1*, 47–63.

Bateson, M. C. (1989). *Composing a life.* New York, NY: The Atlantic Monthly Press.

Baxter Magolda, M. (2001). *Making their own way: Narratives for transforming higher education to promote self-development.* Sterling, VA: Stylus.

Becvar, R., Canfield, B., & Becvar, D. (1997). *Group work: Cybernetic, constructivist, and social constructionist perspectives.* Denver, CO: Love.

Behruzi, R., Hatem, M., Goulet, L., Fraser, W., & Misago, C. (2013). Understanding childbirth practices as an organizational cultural phenomenon: A conceptual framework. *BMC Pregnancy and Childbirth, 13*, 205.

Birkmeyer, J. D., Barnato, A., Birkmeyer, A., Bessler, R., & Skinner, J. (2020). The impact of the COVID-19 pandemic on hospital admissions in the United States. *Health Affairs, 39*(11), 2010–2017.

Bosek, M., Laramie, A., & Hoffman, S. (2021, November). *Providing nursing care as the country continues to experience a pandemic* [Conference presentation]. Nursing Research Evidence-Based Practice Symposium, North Ferrisburgh, VT. www.nursingresearchsym.org/new-page

Bowlby, J. (1980). Loss: Sadness & depression. Attachment and loss (vol. 3); (International psycho-analytical library no.109). London: Hogarth.

Brown, C., & Augusta-Scott, T. (2007). *Narrative therapy: Making meaning, making lives.* Thousand Oaks, CA: Sage.

Bureau of Labor Statistics. (2019). *Consumer expenditures report.* Washington, DC: U.S. Department of Labor. Retrieved from www.bls.gov/opub/reports/consumer-expenditures/2019/home.htm

Bureau of Labor Statistics (2022, February 1). *Job openings and labor turnover summary.* Washington, DC: Author.

Bureau of Labor Statistics, (2022, March 7). *BLS data viewer.* Washington, DC: U.S. Department of Labor. Retrieved from beta.bls.gov/dataViewer/view/timeseries/JTS923000000000000QUR

Bushe, G., & Gibbs, B. (1990). Predicting organization development consulting competence from the Myers-Briggs Type Indicator and stage of ego development. *The Journal of Applied Behavioral Science, 26*(3), 337–357.

Cacioppo, S., Grippo, A., London, S., Goossens, L., & Cacioppo, J. (2015). Loneliness: Clinical import and interventions. *Perspectives on Psychological Science, 10*(2), 238–249. Retrieved from doi.org/10.1177%2F1745691615570616

Carlsen, M. (1988). *Meaning-making: Therapeutic processes in adult development.* New York, NY: W. W. Norton.

Carlsen, M. B. (1991). *Creative aging: A meaning-making perspective.* New York, NY: W. W. Norton.

Cassellius, B. (2022, February 9). *Opinion: My fellow educators are quitting in droves. Here's why.* Washington, DC: The Washington Post.

Center for Violence Prevention. (2021). *Gun violence: Facts and statistics.* Philadelphia, PA: Children's Hospital. Retrieved from violence.chop.edu/gun-violence-facts-and-statistics

Chiari, G., & Nuzzo, M. L. (2010). *Constructivist psychotherapy: A narrative hermeneutic approach.* New York, NY: Routledge.

Children's Defense Fund. (2021, December). *The state of America's children 2021.* Retrieved from www.childrensdefense.org/wp-content/uploads/2021/04/The-State -of-Americas-Children-2021.pdf

Choi, J., Zhu, J., & Goodman, L. (2019). *Young adults living in parents' basements: Causes and consequences.* Washington, DC: Urban Institute.

Cobb-Moore, C., Danby, S., & Farrell, A. (2009). Young children as rule makers. *Journal of Pragmatics, 41,* 1477–1492.

Cooley, C. (1902). *Human nature and the social order,* New York, NY: Charles Scribner's Sons.

COVID Collaborative. (2021, December). Hidden pain: Children who lost a parent or caregiver to COVID-19 and what the nation can do to help them. Retrieved from www.covidcollaborative.us/assets/uploads/img/HIDDEN-PAIN-

Craig, C. J. (2002). A meta-level analysis of the conduit in lives lived and stories told. *Teachers and Teaching: Theory and Practice, 8*(2), 197–221.

Davenport, D. (1981). A closer look at the healthy grieving process. *Personnel & Guidance Journal, 59,* 332–335.

Davis, C., & Nolen-Hoeksema, S. (2001). Loss and meaning: How do people make sense of loss? *American Behavioral Scientist, 44*(5), 726–741.

Davis, C., Wortman, C., Lehman, D., & Silver, R. (2000). Searching for meaning in loss: Are clinical assumptions correct? *Death Studies, 24,* 497–540.

Demos, J., & Demos, V. (1969). Adolescence in historical perspective. *Journal of Marriage and Family, 31,* 632–638.

DeRue, D., & Wellman, N. (2009). Developing leaders via experience: The role of developmental challenge, learning orientation, and feedback availability. *Journal of Applied Psychology, 94*(4), 859–875.

Dewey, J. (1897). My pedagogic creed. *School Journal, 54*(3), 77–80.

Dewey, J. (1933). *How we think* (rev. ed.). Lexington, MA: Heath. (Original work published 1910)

Doka, K. (2008). Disenfranchised grief in historical and cultural perspective. In M. Stroebe, R. Hansson, H. Schut, & W. Stroebe (Eds.), *Handbook of bereavement research and practice: Advances in theory and intervention* (pp. 223–240). Washington, DC: American Psychological Association.

Donovan, D. (2022, May 17). *U. S. officially passes 1 million COVID-19 deaths.* Baltimore, MD: Johns Hopkins University. Retrieved from coronavirus.jhu.edu/

Drago-Severson, E. (2016). Teaching, learning, and leading in today's complex world: Reaching new heights with a developmental approach. *International Journal of Leadership in Education, 19*(1), 56–86.

Elkind, D. (1974). *Children and adolescents* (2nd ed.). New York, NY: Oxford University Press.

Epstein, R. (2010). *Teen 2.0: Saving our children and families from the torment of adolescence*. Fresno, CA: Quill Driver Books.

Erikson, E. (1968). *Identity: Youth and crisis*. New York, NY: W. W. Norton.

Fasick, F. A. (1994). On the "invention" of adolescence. *The Journal of Early Adolescence, 14*(1), 6–23.

Ferreira, J., Basseches, M., & Vasco, A. (2017). Guidelines for reflective practice in psychotherapy: A reflection on the benefits of combining moment-by-moment and phase-by-phase mapping in clinical decision making. *Journal of Psychotherapy Integration, 27*(1), 35–46.

Feuerstein, R. (1979). *The dynamic assessment of retarded performers: The learning potential assessment device, theory, instruments, and techniques*. Baltimore, MD: University Park Press.

Franz, J. L. E. (2021, November 11). *What's it really like to be a nurse during a pandemic?* College of Nursing and Health Science, University of Vermont. Retrieved from www.uvm.edu/news/cnhs/whats-it-really-be-nurse-during-pandemic

Freeman, M. (2015). Paradoxes of the constructed: Narrative psychology and beyond. In J. Raskin, S. Bridges, & J. Kahn (Eds.), *Studies in meaning 5: Perturbing the status quo in constructivist psychology* (pp. 119–151). New York, NY: Pace University Press.

Ghosh, R., Haynes, R., & Kram, K. (2013). Developing networks at work: Holding environments for leader development. *Career Development International, 18*(3), 232–256.

Gibson, C., & McDaniel, D. (2010). Moving beyond conventional wisdom: Advancements in cross-cultural theories of leadership, conflict, and teams. Perspectives on Psychological Science, 5(4), 450–462.

Gilbert, A., & Sliep, Y. (2009). Reflexivity in the practice of social action: From self- to inter-relational reflexivity. *South African Journal of Psychology, 39*(4), 468–479.

Gilligan, C. (1982). *In a different voice: Psychological theory and women's development*. Cambridge, MA: Harvard University Press.

Goldman, L. (2013). *Life and loss: A guide to help grieving children* (3rd ed.). New York: NY: Routledge.

Gun Violence Archive. (2021, December). [Gun violence archive 2021]. Retrieved from www.gunviolencearchive.org

Hansen, J. T. (2006). Counseling theories within a postmodernist epistemology: New roles for theories in counseling practice. *Journal of Counseling & Development, 84*, 291–297.

Hardecker, S., Schmidt, M., & Tomasello, M. (2016). Children's developing understanding of the conventionality of rules. *Journal of Cognition and Development, 18*,163–188.

Harris, D. (2011). *Counting our losses: Reflecting on change, loss, and transition in everyday life*. New York, NY: Routledge.

Harter, S. (2012). *The construction of the self* (2nd ed.). New York, NY: Guilford.

Hauser, S. (1983). Ego development and self-image complexity in early adolescence. *Archives of General Psychiatry, 40*, 325–332.

Hawkins, S., Yudkin, D., Juan-Torres, M., & Dixon, T. (2018). *Hidden tribes: A study of America's polarized landscape.* New York, NY: More in Common.

Hayes, R. L. (1981). High school graduation: The case for identity loss. *Personnel & Guidance Journal, 59,* 369–371.

Hayes, R. L. (1984). Coping with loss: A developmental approach to helping children and youth. *Counseling and Human Development, 17*(3), 1–12.

Hayes, R. L. (2020). *Making meaning: A constructivist approach to counseling and groupwork in education.* Lanham, MD: Lexington Books.

Heifetz, R., & Linsky, M. (2004). When leadership spells danger. *Educational Leadership, 61*(7), 33–37.

Heine, S. (2011). *Cultural psychology.* New York, NY: Norton.

Helsing, D., Howell, A., Kegan, R., & Lahey, L. (2008). Putting the "development" in professional development: Understanding and overturning educational leaders' immunities to change. *Harvard Educational Review, 78*(3), 437–465.

Hendricks, G., & Weinhold, B. (1982). *Transpersonal approaches to counseling and psychotherapy.* Denver, CO: Love.

Henrich, N. J., Dodek, P. M., Alden, L., Keenan, S. P., & Rodney, P. (2016). Causes of moral distress in the intensive care unit: A qualitative study. *Journal of Critical Care, 35,* 57–62.

Hewlett, B. (Ed.). (2013). *Adolescent identity: Evolutionary, cultural and developmental perspectives.* New York, NY: Routledge.

Holland, J. M., Currier, J. M., & Neimeyer, R. A. (2006). Meaning reconstruction in the first two years of bereavement: The role of sense-making and benefit-finding. *Omega: Journal of Death and Dying, 53*(3), 175–191.

Holland, J. M., & Neimeyer, R. A. (2010). An examination of stage theory of grief among individuals bereaved by natural and violent causes: A meaning-oriented contribution. *OMEGA, 61*(2), 103–120.

James, W. (1890). *The principles of psychology.* New York, NY: Holt, Rinehart & Winston.

Janoff-Bulman, R., & Frantz, C. (1997). The impact of trauma on meaning: From meaningless world to meaningful life. In M. Power & C. Brewin (Eds.), *The transformation of meaning in psychological therapies: Integrating theory and practice* (pp. 91–106). Hoboken, NJ: Wiley.

Janov, I. (1970). *The primal scream.* New York: NY: Dell.

Jensen, P. (2007). On learning from experience: Personal and private experiences as the context for psychotherapeutic practice. *Clinical Child Psychology and Psychiatry, 12*(3), 375–384.

Joseph, S., & Linley, P. (2005). Positive adjustment to threatening events: An organismic valuing theory of growth through adversity. *Review of General Psychology, 9,* 262–280.

Journal of Adolescence. (2018, May 19). Introduction. *Author.* Retrieved from www .elsevier.com/journals/journal-of-adolescence/0140-1971/guide-for-authors

Karp, D. A. (1988). A decade of reminders: Changing age consciousness between fifty and sixty years old. *The Gerontologist, 28*(6), 727–738.

Kauffman, J. (Ed.). (2002). *Loss of the assumptive world.* New York, NY: Brunner-Routledge.

Kegan, R. (1982). *The evolving self: Problem and process in human development.* Cambridge, MA: Harvard University Press.

Kegan, R. (1994). *In over our heads: The mental demands of modern life.* Cambridge, MA: Harvard University Press.

Kegan, R. (2000). What "form" transforms? A constructive-developmental approach to transformative learning. In J. Mezirow (Ed.), *Learning as transformation* (pp. 35–69). San Francisco, CA: Jossey-Bass.

Kegan, R., & Lahey, L. (2009). *Immunity to change: How to overcome it and unlock the potential in yourself and your organization.* Brighton, MA: Harvard Business Review Press.

Kegan, R., & Lahey, L. (2016). *An everyone culture: Becoming a deliberately developmental organization.* Boston, MA: Harvard Business Review Press.

Keniston, K. (1970). Youth: A "new" stage of life. *American Scholar, 39,* 631–641.

Kenyon, B. (2001). Current research in children's conceptions of death: A critical review. *Journal of Death and Dying, 43*(10), 63–91.

Klaus, M., & Kennell, J. (1976). *Maternal-infant bonding.* St. Louis, MO: Mosby.

Knapp, S., Gottlieb, M. C., & Handelsman, M. M. (2017). Enhancing professionalism through self-reflection. *Professional Psychology: Research and Practice, 48*(3), 167–174.

Kohlberg, L. (1969). Stage and sequence: The cognitive-developmental approach to socialization. In D. Goslin (Ed.)., *Handbook of socialization theory and research* (pp. 347–480). Chicago, IL: Rand McNally.

Koocher, G. (1973). Childhood, death, and cognitive development. *Developmental Psychology, 9,* 369–375.

Kraus, B. (2015). The life we live and the life we experience: Introducing the epistemological difference between "Lifeworld" (Lebenswelt) and "Life Conditions" (Lebenslage). *Social Work and Society. International Online Journal, 13*(2). Retrieved from www.socwork.net/sws/article/view/438/816

Krauss, S. (2005). Research paradigms and meaning-making: A primer. *The Qualitative Report, 10*(4), 758–770. Retrieved from nova.edu/sss/QR/QR10–4/krauss.pdf

Krepia, M., Krepia, V., & Tsilingiri, M. (2017). School children's perception of the concept of death. *International Journal of Caring Sciences, 10,* 1717–1720.

Kubler-Ross, E. (1969). *On death and dying.* New York, NY: Macmillan.

Kubler-Ross, E., & Kessler, D. (2014). *On grief and grieving: Finding the meaning of grief through the five stages of loss.* New York, NY: Charles Scribner's Sons.

Lachman, M., Teshale, S., & Arigoroaei, S. (2015). Midlife as a pivotal period in the life course: Balancing growth and decline at the crossroads of youth and old age. *International Journal of Behavioral Development, 39*(1), 20–31.

Langa, K. M., Larson, E. B., Crimmins, E. M., Faul, J. D., Levine, D. A., Kabeto, M. U., & Weir, D. R. (2017). A comparison of the prevalence of dementia in the United States in 2000 and 2012. *JAMA Internal Medicine, 177,* 51–58.

Lapsley, D. (1993). Toward an integrated theory of adolescent ego development: The "new look" at adolescent egocentrism. *American Journal of Orthopsychiatry, 63*(4), 562–571.

Larkin, R. (2009). The Columbine legacy: Rampage shootings as political acts. *American Behavioral Scientist, 52,* 1309–1326.

Larson, D. (1993). *The helper's journey: Working with people facing grief, loss, and life-threatening illness.* Champaign, IL: Research Press.

Lauro, S. (Ed.). (2017). *Zombie theory: A reader.* Minneapolis, MN: University of Minnesota Press. Retrieved from www.jstor.org/stable/10.5749/j.ctt1pwt6zr

Le Boyer, F. (1975). *Birth without violence.* New York, NY: Knopf.

Lepore, S., Wortman, C., Silver, R., & Wayment, H. (1996). Social constraints, intrusive thoughts, and depressive symptoms among bereaved mothers. *Journal of Personality and Social Psychology, 70*(2), 271–282.

Lerner, R., & Steinberg, L. (Eds.). (2009). *Handbook of adolescent psychology* (3rd ed., Vol. 1). New York, NY: Wiley.

Levinson, D. (1978). *The seasons of a man's life.* New York, NY: Ballantine.

Lewis, C. S. (1964). *A grief observed.* London, England: Faber & Faber. (Original work published under the pseudonym N. W. Clark, 1961)

Long, C. (2021, August 23). Educator anxiety rises with COVID surge. *NEA Today.* Washington, DC: National Education Association.

Luong, G., Arredondo, C. M., & Charles, S. T. (2020). Cultural differences in coping with interpersonal tensions lead to divergent shorter- and longer-term affective consequences. *Cognition and Emotion, 34*(7), 1499–1508.

Manners, J., Durkin, K., & Nesdale, A. (2004). Promoting advanced ego development among adults. *Journal of Adult Development, 11*(1), 19–27.

Marris, P. (1986). *Loss and change* (rev. ed). London, England: Routledge and Kegan Paul.

Martens, M. L. (2009). A comparison of stress factors in home and inpatient hospice nurses. *Journal of Hospice and Palliative Nursing, 11,* 144–153.

Maturana, H., & Varela, F. (1992). *The tree of knowledge: The biological roots of human understanding* (rev. ed.; R. Paolucci, Trans.). Boston: Shambhala. Retrieved from www.cybertech-engineering.ch/research/references/Maturana1988/maturana-h-1987-tree-of-knowledge-bkmrk.pdf

McCabe, M. (2003). *The paradox of loss: Toward a relational theory of grief.* Westport, CT: Praeger Publishers/Greenwood Publishing Group.

McCrae, R. R. (2004). Openness to experience. In C. D. Spielberger (Ed.), *Encyclopedia of Applied Psychology* (pp. 707–709). Cambridge, MA: Academic Press/Elsevier.

McDevitt, T., & Ormrod, J. (2019). *Child development and education* (7th ed.). Hoboken, NJ: Pearson.

McEwen, B. S. (1998). Protective and damaging effects of stress mediators. *New England Journal of Medicine, 338*(3), 171–179.

Mead, G. H. (1934). *Mind, self, and society.* Chicago, IL: University of Chicago Press.

Meier, E. A., Gallegos, J. V., Thomas, L. P., Depp, C. A., Irwin, S. A., & Jeste, D. V. (2016). Defining a good death (successful dying): Literature review and a call for research and public dialogue. *The American Journal of Geriatric Psychiatry, 24*(4), 261–271.

Merrimack College. (2022). *First annual Merrimack College teacher survey: 2022 results.* Bethesda, MD: Education Week Research. Retrieved from www.edweek .org/products/todays-teachers-are-deeply-disillusioned-survey-data-confirms

Merron, K., Fisher, D., & Torbert, W. (1987). Meaning making and management action. *Group & Organization Studies, 12*(3), 274–286.

Mezirow, J. (2000). Learning to think like an adult: Core concepts of transformation theory. In J. Mezirow and Associates (Eds.), *Learning as transformation: Critical perspectives on a theory in progress* (pp. 3–33). San Francisco, CA: Jossey-Bass.

Miller, A. (1976). *Death of a salesman.* New York, NY: Penguin Plays. (Original work published 1949)

Miron, O., Yu, K., Wilf-Miron, R., & Kohane, I. (2019). Suicide rates among adolescents and young adults in the United States, 2000–2017. *Journal of the American Medical Association, 321*(23), 2362–2364.

Mitchell, J. (1970). Big yellow taxi. On *Ladies of the canyon*, Reprise.

Montgomery, L. M. (1908). *Anne of Green Gables.* Boston, MA: L. C. Page and Co.

Murman D. L. (2015). The Impact of Age on Cognition. *Seminars in Hearing, 36*(3), 111–121. doi.org/10.1055/s-0035–1555115

Nagy, M. (1948). The child's theories concerning death. *Journal of Genetic Psychology, 73,* 3–27.

National Association of School Psychologists. (2015). *Recommended books for children coping with loss or trauma.* Bethesda, MD: Author.

National Restaurant Association. (2022, February 1). *2022 State of the restaurant industry report.* Washington, DC: Author.

Neimeyer, R. (Ed.). (2001). *Meaning reconstruction and the experience of loss.* Washington, DC: American Psychological Association.

Neimeyer, R., Burke, L., Mackay, M., & van Dyke Stringer, J. (2010). Grief therapy and the reconstruction of meaning: From principles to practice. *Journal of Contemporary Psychotherapy, 40*(2), 73–83.

Nelson, L., & Barry, C. (2005). Distinguishing features of emerging adulthood: The role of self-classification as an adult. *Journal of Adolescent Research, 20,* 242–262.

Neubert, S. (2009). Pragmatism, constructivism, and the theory of culture. In L. Hickman, S. Neubert, & K. Reich (Eds.), *John Dewey: Between pragmatism and constructivism* (pp. 162–184). New York, NY: Fordham University Press.

New York Life Foundation/National Alliance for Children's Grief. (2021). *Childhood Bereavement Estimation Model.* Retrieved from childrengrieve.org/awareness/ childhood-bereavement-estimation-model-cbem

O'Connor, T., Allen, J., Bell, K., & Hauser, S. (1996). Adolescent–parent relationships and leaving home in young adulthood. In J. Graber & J. Dubas (Eds.), *New directions for child development*, No. 71. *Leaving home: Understanding the transition to adulthood* (pp. 39–52). San Francisco, CA: Jossey-Bass.

Office for Civil Rights. (2021, June 9). *Education in a pandemic: The disparate impacts of COVID-19 on America's students.* Washington, DC: U.S. Department of Education. Retrieved from www2.ed.gov/about/offices/list/ocr/docs/20210608 -impacts-of-covid19.pdf

Oltjenbruns, K. (2001). Developmental context of childhood: Grief and regrief phenomena. In M. Stroebe, R. Hansson, W. Stroebe, & H. Schut (Eds.), *Handbook of bereavement research: Consequences, coping, and care* (pp. 169–197). Washington, DC: American Psychological Association.

Overton, W., & Muller, U. (2013). Metatheories, theories, and concepts in the study of development. In I. Weiner, R. Lerner, M. Easterbrooks, & J. Mistry (Eds.), *Handbook of psychology* (2nd ed.), Volume 6, *Developmental psychology I, Foundations of development across the life span* (pp. 10–49). Hoboken, NJ: Wiley.

Park, C. (2010). Making sense of the meaning literature: An integrative review of meaning making and its effects on adjustment to stressful life events. *Psychological Bulletin, 136*(2), 257–301.

Parkes, C. M., Laungani, P., & Young, W. (Eds.). (1996). *Death and bereavement across cultures.* London, England: Routledge.

Pearce, J. (1977). *The magical child: Rediscovering nature's plan for our children.* New York, NY: E. Dutton.

Perlman, D. (1990, August 10–14). *Age difference in loneliness: A meta-analysis* [Paper presentation]. American Psychological Association, Boston, MA. Retrieved from files.eric.ed.gov/fulltext/ED326767.pdf

Perry, W. (1970). *Forms of intellectual and ethical development in the college years.* New York, NY: Holt, Rinehart & Winston.

Piaget, J. (1954). *The origins of intelligence in children.* New York, NY: International Universities Press. (Original work published 1936)

Piaget, J. (1955). *The language and thought of the child.* Cleveland, OH: World Publishing. (Original work published 1926)

Piaget, J. (1965). *The moral judgment of the child.* Glencoe, IL: Free Press. (Original work published 1932).

Pride, R. (2002). *The political use of racial narratives: School desegregation in Mobile, Alabama, 1954–1997.* Chicago, IL: University of Illinois Press.

Prince, M., Albanese, E., Guerchet, M., & Prina, M. (2014). *Dementia and risk reduction: An analysis of protective and modifiable factors.* London, England: Alzheimer's Disease International.

Qualter, P., Vanhalst, J., Harris, R., Van Roekel, E., Lodder, G., Bangee, M., Maes, M., & Verhagen, M. (2015). Loneliness across the life span. *Perspectives on Psychological Science, 10*(2), 250–264.

Quote Investigator. (October, 2010). *Mark Twain? Apocryphal?* Retrieved from quoteinvestigator.com/2010/10/10/twain-father/

Rappaport, J. (2000). Community narratives: Tales of terror and joy. *American Journal of Community Psychology, 28*, 1–24.

Raskin, J. (2015). An introductory perturbation: What is constructivism and is there a future in it? In J. Raskin, S. Bridges, & J. Kahn (Eds.), *Studies in meaning 5:*

Perturbing the status quo in constructivist psychology (pp. 3–27). New York, NY: Pace University Press.

Ray, S., & Davidson, S. (2014). *Dementia and cognitive decline: A review of the evidence.* London, England: Age UK. Retrieved from www.ageuk.org.uk /globalassets/age-uk/documents/reports-and-publications/reports-and-briefings/ health--wellbeing/rb_oct14_cognitive_decline_and_dementia_evidence_review _age_uk.pdf

Reilly, K. (2020, August 26). *This is what it's like to be a teacher during the coronavirus pandemic.* New York, NY: Time. Retrieved from time.com/5883384/teachers-coronavirus/

Reinhart, R. J. (2020, January 6). *Nurses continue to rate highest in honesty, ethics.* Retrieved from news.gallup.com/poll/274673/ nurses-continue-rate-highest-honesty-ethics.aspx

Rest, J., Turiel, E., & Kohlberg, L. (1969). Level of moral development as a determinant of preference and comprehension of moral judgments made by others. *Journal of Personality, 37*(2), 225–252.

Riegel, K. (1979). *Foundations of dialectical psychology.* San Diego, CA: Academic Press.

Rodgers, C., & Scott, K. (2008). The development of the personal self and professional identity in learning to teach. In M. Cochran-Smith, S. Feiman-Nemser, D. McIntyre, & K. Demers (Eds.), *Handbook of research on teacher education* (pp. 732–755). New York, NY: Routledge.

Rose, R. (1955). *Twelve angry men.* Chicago, IL: The Dramatic Publishing Company.

Schachtel, E. (1959). *Metamorphosis.* New York, NY: Basic Books.

Schon, D. (1987). *Educating the reflective practitioner.* San Francisco, CA: Jossey-Bass.

Schulz, K. (2022, January 22). How to make sense of our COVID losses, big and small. *The New York Times.* Retrieved from www.nytimes.com/2022/01/25/opinion /pandemic-grief-loss.html

Schwartz, S. J., Salas-Wright, C. P., Pérez-Gómez, A., Mejía-Trujillo, J., Brown, E. C., Montero-Zamora, P., Meca, A., Scaramutti, C., Soares, M. H., Vos, S. R., Javakhishvili, N., & Dickson-Gomez, J. (2018). Cultural stress and psychological symptoms in recent Venezuelan immigrants to the United States and Colombia. *International Journal of Intercultural Relations, 67*, 25–34.

Shechter, A., Diaz, F., Moise, N., Anstey, D., Ye, S., Agarwal, S., Birk, J., Brodie, D., Cannone, D., Chang, B., Claassen, J., Cornelius, T., Derby, L., Dong, M., Givens, R., Hochman, B., Homma, S., Kronish, I., Lee, S., Manzano, W., . . . Abdalla, M. (2020). Psychological distress, coping behaviors, and preferences for support among New York healthcare workers during the COVID-19 pandemic. *General Hospital Psychiatry, 66*, 1–8.

Siegler, R., Saffron, J., Gershoff, E., Eisenberg, N., DeLoache, J., & Leaper, C. (2017). *How children develop* (5th ed.). New York, NY: Worth Publishers.

Sinnott, J. D., & Guttman, D. (1978). Piagetian logical abilities and older adults' abilities to solve everyday problems. *Human Development, 21*(5/6), 327–333.

Sinsky, C. A., Brown, R. L., Stillman, M. J., & Linzer, M. (2021). *COVID-Related stress and work intentions in a sample of U.S. health care workers.* Oxford, England: Elsevier.

Spatz, D. (2004, January 18). Faking Carlin: Internet entries are not his work. *Chicago Daily Herald,* p. 17.

Spiegel, Y. (1977). *The grief process: Analysis and counseling.* Nashville, TN: Abingdon.

Springer, C., & Wallerstein, J. (1983, March). Young adolescents' responses to their parents' divorces. In L. A. Kurdeck (Ed.), Children and divorce. *New Directions for Child Development, 19,* pp. 15–27. San Francisco, CA: Jossey-Bass.

Steiner, E. D., & Woo, A. (2021). *Job-related stress threatens the teacher supply: Key findings from the 2021 State of the U.S. Teacher Survey.* Santa Monica, CA: RAND Corporation.

Stockton, A., & King, L. (2021, February 24). Death through a nurse's eyes [Video file]. Retrieved from www.nytimes.com/video/opinion/100000007578176/covid-icu-nurses-arizona.html

Storr, W. (2018). *Selfie: How we became so self-obsessed and what it's doing to us.* New York, NY: Overlook Press.

Strang, S., & Kuhnert, K. (2009). Personality and leadership development levels as predictors of leader performance. *Leadership Quarterly, 20*(3), 421–433.

Stroebe, M., Hansson, R., Schut, H., & Stroebe, W. (2008). *Handbook of bereavement research and practice: Advances in theory and intervention.* Washington, DC: American Psychological Association.

Stillion, J., & Attig, T. (Eds.). (2015). *Death, dying, and bereavement: Contemporary perspectives, institutions and practices.* New York, NY: Springer.

Syed, M., Santos, C., Yoo, H., & Juang, L. (2018). Invisibility of racial/ethnic minorities in developmental science: Implications for research and institutional practices. *American Psychologist, 73*(6), 812–826.

Szabo, J. (2009). *Death and dying: An annotated bibliography of the thanatological literature.* Lanham, MD: Scarecrow Press.

Tanner, T. (1971). *City of words: American fiction, 1950–1970.* New York, NY: Harper & Row.

Taylor, S. (1983). Adjustment to threatening events: A theory of cognitive adaptation. *American Psychologist, 38*(11), 1161–1173.

Terracciano, A., Abdel-Khalek, A., Adam, N., Adamovova, L., Akn, H., Alansari, M., Alcalay, L., Allik, J., Angleienet, A., Avia, A., Auearst, L., Babaranelli, C., Beer, A., Borg-Cunen, M., Bratko, D., Brunner-Sciarra, M., Budzinski, L., Camart, N., Dahourou, D., et al. (2005). National character does not reflect mean personality trait level in 49 cultures. *Science, 310*(5745), 96–100.

Thornicroft, G. (2021, December). Exploring the global consequences of the COVID-19 pandemic. *Psychiatric Times, 38*(12). Retrieved from www.psychiatrictimes.com/view/exploring-the-global-consequences-of-the-covid19-pandemic

Torbert, W. (1994). Cultivating postformal adult development: Higher stages and contrasting interventions. In M. Miller, M., & S. Cook-Greuter (Eds.), *Transcendence and mature thought in adulthood: The further reaches of human development* (pp. 181–203). Lanham, MD: Rowman & Littlefield.

Treglia, D., Cutuli, J. J., Arasteh, K., J. Bridgeland, J.M., Edson, G., Phillips, S., Balakrishna, A. (2021, December). *Hidden pain: Children who lost a parent or caregiver to COVID-19 and what the nation can do to help them.* Washington, DC: COVID Collaborative. Retrieved from www.covidcollaborative.us/assets/uploads/img/HIDDEN-PAIN-FINAL.pdf

Triandis, H. (2001). Individualism-collectivism and personality. *Journal of Pesonality, 69*, 907–924.

Truluck, J. E., & Courtenay, B. C. (2002). Ego development and the influence of gender, age, and educational levels among older adults. *Educational Gerontology, 28*(4), 325–336.

Twain, M. (1876). *The Adventures of Tom Sawyer.* Hartford, CT: American Publishing Co.

UNICEF (2021, October). The state of the world's children 2021: *On my mind: Promoting, protecting and caring for children's mental health.* Retrieved from www.unicef.org/reports/state-worlds-children-2021

U.S. Census Bureau. (2019, November). Median age at first marriage: 1890 to present. *Decennial Censuses, 1890 to 1940, and Current Population Survey, Annual Social and Economic Supplements, 1947 to 2018.* Washington, DC: Author. Retrieved from www.census.gov/content/dam/Census/library/visualizations/time-series/demo/families-and-households/ms-2.pdf

U.S. Census Bureau. (2018, March 13). Older people projected to outnumber children for first time in U.S. history. Washington, DC: Author. Retrieved from www.census.gov/newsroom/press-releases/2018/cb18-41-population-projections.html

Vaillant, G., & McCullough, L. (1987). The Washington University Sentence Completion Test compared with other measures of adult ego development. *American Journal of Psychiatry, 144*(9), 1189–1194.

Vernon, A. (2002). *What works when with children and adolescents: A handbook of individual counseling techniques.* Champaign, IL: Research Press.

von Glasersfeld, E. (1984). An introduction to radical constructivism. In P. Watzlawick (Ed.), *The invented reality: How do we know what we believe we know: Contributions to constructivism* (pp. 17–40). New York, NY: Norton.

Vygotsky, L. S. (1978). *Mind in society: The development of higher psychological properties.* Cambridge, MA: Harvard University Press.

Watzlawick, P. (1984). *The invented reality: Contributions to constructivism.* New York, NY: Norton.

Weenolsen, P. (1988). *Transcendence of loss over the life span.* New York. NY: Hemisphere.

Werner, H. (1957). The concept of development from a comparative and organismic point of view. In D. Harris (Ed.), *The concept of development.* Minneapolis, MN: University of Minnesota Press.

Wheat, L., & Whiting, P. (2018). Sacred privilege: Using narrative reconstruction as a postmodern approach with grieving children and adolescents. In M. Scholl & J. Hansen (Eds.), *Postmodern perspectives on contemporary counseling issues: Approaches across diverse settings* (pp. 93–120). New York, NY: Oxford University Press.

Winokuer, H., & Harris, D. (2016). *Principles and practices of grief counseling* (2nd ed.). New York, NY: Springer.

Winnicott, D. W. (2002). *Winnicott on the Child.* Cambridge, MA: Perseus.

Wood, D., Bruner, J., & Ross, G. (1976). The role of tutoring in problem solving. *Journal of Child Psychology and Psychiatry, 17*, 89–100.

Worden, J. (2018). *Grief counseling and grief therapy* (5th ed.). New York, NY: Springer.

World Health Organization. (2017). *Depression and other common mental disorders: Global health estimates.* Geneva, Switzerland: Author.

Index

About the Author

Richard L. Hayes is professor emeritus of the University of Georgia and dean emeritus of the University of South Alabama. A Harvard College graduate, he received his master's and doctorate from Boston University. A former public school teacher and counselor, he has held additional faculty positions at Colgate University and Bradley University and has been a visiting faculty member at the University of Tokyo, Japan; the University of Jyvaskyla, Finland; the University of Salamanca, Spain; and the University of Glasgow, Scotland. He is a past president of the Association for Moral Education and the Association for Specialists in Group Work and is a fellow in the American Educational Research Association, the American Psychological Association, and the Association for Specialists in Group Work. He is currently a counseling psychologist with The Hayes Group in Athens, GA.